𝒫RAYER 𝒢UIDE
FOR THE
𝐵ROKENHEARTED

OTHER BOOKS BY
MICHELLE MCKINNEY HAMMOND

What To Do Until Love Finds You
Secrets of an Irresistible Woman
The Genius of Temptation
His Love Always Finds Me
The Power of Femininity
Get A Love Life
If Men Are Like Buses Then How Do I Catch One?

To correspond with Ms. McKinney Hammond, write to:
HeartWing Ministries
P.O. Box 11052
Chicago, Ill. 60611

or email her at <u>heartwingmin@yahoo.com</u>

For speaking engagement enquiries contact:
Speak Up Speaker Services
1(888)870-7719

Ladies, be as determined to get information as you are to embrace anything that is important to you. If your local bookstores do not have these books in stock, they are always happy to order them for you. When all else fails, there's always Amazon.com. Happy reading!

PRAYER GUIDE
for the
BROKENHEARTED

Comfort and Healing
on the Way to Wholeness

Michelle McKinney Hammond

SERVANT PUBLICATIONS
ANN ARBOR, MICHIGAN

Vine Books is an imprint of Servant Publications especially designed to serve evangelical Christians.

Published by Servant Publications
P.O. Box 8617
Ann Arbor, Michigan 48107

Cover photograph: Bob Foran, Ann Arbor, Michigan
Cover design: Alan Furst, Minneapolis, Minnesota

03   10 9 8 7 6

Printed in the United States of America
ISBN 1-56955-222-3

$\mathcal{D}$edication

To my loving parents, who have wiped my knees
every time I've scraped them.

Mr. & Mrs. William & Norma McKinney
Mr. & Mrs. George & Charity Hammond

To my Heavenly Father, who has wiped my tears
every time others have scraped my spirit.
Father, you have watched me scrambling to retrieve
the pieces of my broken heart more times than I need
to mention. That is our secret. But your power to heal is not.
Thank you for making me whole again.

I never thought I'd say this, but to all of the men in my life
from whom I've learned lessons the hard way. Thank you for
contributing to my ability to comfort others
with the comfort that I have received.

Acknowledgements

To my new friends at Servant Publications. I thank you. Thank you for this book. You'll never know what it has meant to have the opportunity to write this.

Bert Ghezzi, I am so glad you are a determined man.

Heidi Hess Saxton, my editor, thank you for your encouragement, the uplifting notes, and your focus. I couldn't have finished this without you.

Sheila Frazier and Dee Dee Garlington ... whew! God bless you two! If I could pay you for the buckets of tears you collected from me over the years while I processed all my stuff, you'd be wealthy women. Instead I am the one who has been made wealthy by your sisterhood. Thank you for sticking with me and knowing when to tell me to snap out of it.

Brenda, Michelle, Theresa, Denise, Peggy, Bunny, Terri, Nancy, Cindy, Karen, Charlotte, Jan, Charlot, Susan, Jacqueline, and Nicole. I sure am blessed to have had you spotting me over the years. I might have "fallen off the trampoline" if it weren't for your ears, your prayers, your sound advice, and your relentless determination to keep me accountable.

I don't think anyone could have a more wonderful inner circle of sisters in the spirit!

You know what, ladies? Over the years we've all come a mighty long way.

Contents

$\mathcal{I}$ntroduction
∞

$\mathcal{S}$o ... You've had your cry. You have vented to everyone who would listen. You might have even called him and hung up a few times. Or maybe you have not had the courage to sever the ties that bind out of fear of the unknown. You find yourself stuck in your pain....

All right, take a deep breath. We are about to turn the corner.

Yes, everyone is entitled to grieve for a time. It's the natural order of things. However, we must not remain in the valley of weeping. You'll find if you do, you'll drown everything but your sorrows.

How do you move forward? You make a decision to move on. Against every instinct. Feeling. Gut reaction. Even the advice of a few misguided friends. You move on. Pick a day to end the drama and turn the channel on your heart to a new program.

Though someone was responsible for ruining your yesterday, you possess the power to be responsible for your tomorrows. You can rewrite the script and pick any ending you choose.

So it's entirely up to you. Choose joy. Choose a new beginning. Choose to live life to the fullest again. Without him. Without the pain. Without the memories ... And believe me, you will get by with a little help from one very special friend....

Yes, girlfriend, it is totally up to you.

The Pain

*M*ention the word "heartbreak," and the instant response of most people is compassion. Even from strangers. Everyone has been there some time. We've all loved and lost someone or something that was precious and dear. Whether it was a schoolgirl crush or a mature commitment, love, loss, and disappointment are not foreign to anyone.

Because we are all made in the image of Love itself, the foremost need in the heart of every man and woman is to give and receive love. When that flow is disrupted by rejection or betrayal, our spirits are rent with an excruciating anguish that can rob us of our joy, our peace, our hope for tomorrow.

The Christian's dilemma is this: how do you deal with heartbreak without compromising faith? How do you find the place of peace when your way is blurred with tears?

Other hard questions follow. What do you say to God when your distress renders you speechless? Is God offended by your depression? Does he really understand? And if he really loves you, why didn't he protect your heart in the first place? How could anything good come out of such a bleak situation?

Though everyone has shared the experience of love gone wrong, each situation is extremely personal. Heartbreak comes in all shapes and sizes, colors and shades. One person's irritation is another's torment. Each heart responds to a transgression differently, each suffers by varying degrees. Still, a common denominator remains: heartbreak hurts.

No one can truly know how you feel but you. Others can sympathize, but still you feel alone, trapped inside of your own misery. Will the pain ever end? Will the wounds ever heal? Will you ever dare to love again?

The answer to all of these questions is *yes, yes,* and again I say *yes!*

Though healing is imminent, the process of restoration cannot be avoided. The journey to the mountaintop is always preceded by a walk through the valley. It is the way of the cross. There is no avoiding it, for all who pass this way must take this course.

So allow yourself to feel. Allow yourself to cry and to grieve over your loss. Allow yourself to be angry. But don't allow yourself to be separated from the One who will never leave you or forsake you. If ever there was a time to draw close to God, it's now.

Are you struggling with how to reconcile the tumult of your heart? This book is for you. They say that misery loves company. So allow me to take your hand and walk with you. Perhaps together we can reach beyond your present circumstance to a place of grace and glory. A place of wholeness. A place where love lives and embraces you completely.

I feel like crying
    but the tears won't come
        what's the use of trying when I know that you are gone
            you came and went and all that's left
                are broken pieces of my heart....
Memories of laughter
    echo through my empty room
        suddenly they shatter to reveal an open wound
            just broken pieces of a discarded heart
                broken pieces cut deep and leave their mark
            broken pieces lying on the floor
            broken pieces that can't be mended anymore....
That's the price of living
    when you love someone so hard
        that you can't stop giving
            guess I wasn't very smart
        you threw my heart against the wall
        and watched it breaking from the fall....
Guess it doesn't matter
    it was just a heart to you
        an empty present that someone gave to you
            a nameless owner
        what am I supposed to do
    with broken pieces....

– 1 –

Separation

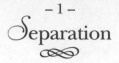

*But the Lord God called to the man, "**Where** are you?"*
GENESIS 3:9

In the midst of a glorious afternoon, a sharp pain entered the heart of God. The arrow flew effortlessly. Past his magnificent surroundings. Past the worship of those continually adoring him with cries of "Holy, Holy." It penetrated deep, slicing through his garments before finding its mark—the center of his heart.

He arose to go in the direction of the intrusion. Down, down he descended, searching for the object of his affection. The one to whom he had given his all, to whom he had imparted his very spirit when he breathed into him the breath of life. This man that he had lovingly caressed as he molded and shaped him into his own image.

Yes, God had given Adam all that he was and all that he had. It was an incredible investment of his omnipotent heart and soul. But something was wrong. Something had changed between them. So God came down to confirm face-to-face what he already knew.

The garden was strangely silent as all of nature held its breath, waiting to see how this drama would unfold. They, too, were aware that something had changed. The atmosphere was pregnant with foreboding. God's countenance suggested that the sweet fellowship and communion he usually shared with the man and woman were not to be this evening. And why were Adam and Eve hiding? Adam usually awaited the Lord's visitation anxiously, as one awaited someone passionately beloved. Yes, something was truly wrong.

The air cooled as if the sun was holding its breath. God spoke, calling gently to Adam. And Adam came forward with the look of an unfaithful lover caught in the act, struggling to shield his guilt from the One who had always been faithful. The moment that Adam had chosen to sin by partaking of the fruit that God had warned against, he chose to snatch his heart out of God's hands and to separate himself from the One who loved him most....

❧

Nothing hurts as deeply as when the one you love chooses to wrench his heart from your grasp, turning his back on the love you so freely gave. Oh, the pain of it, to find that the one you loved prefers another. You have poured out your heart like liquid for another to drink, only to have this valuable libation spilled onto the dust. You offered your choicest treasure, not realizing that your diamonds would be cast to the wind or crushed underfoot, leaving you scrambling to recover the grains and pray for restoration.

This one assurance remains, that God is well acquainted with our grief. He was the first to experience this deep wounding, this tearing separation. He knows how deep the pain can go, and he is prepared to touch our pain and heal it. For while our hearts bleed when those we've loved turn away from us ... it was Jesus' heart that originally bled. Because his heart was broken, ours will mend. As we become vulnerable to his touch, as we learn to trust his advances, we miraculously find that we recover. Though we thought it impossible, we are able to love again.

Dear Heavenly Father, it is so costly to love. I find myself bankrupt, after having spent so much of myself. The one I loved has hidden himself from me, leaving me to search for the shattered pieces of my heart. Help me to recover them from the dust. And as my spirit weeps over my emptiness, please catch my tears and refresh me with them.

I feel naked and ashamed in the face of such rejection. Please dress me with your love and warm me from the cold of my disappointment. As I shiver in my fear of the future, grant me your reassurance that it is you who truly hold the fulfillment of my tomorrows. Help my unbelief and free me from my despair. Restore my deferred hopes and direct my gaze back to you. Back to the center of where true love abides.

When another does not love me as I had hoped, help me to find myself in you. Forgive me for preferring another, for greedily consuming fruit that is not as sweet as you. Heal me and join me to yourself, that I might once again be whole, in Jesus' name. Amen.

Rejection

So Abraham rose early in the morning, and took bread and a
*skin of water and gave them to **Hagar**, putting them on*
her shoulder, and gave her the boy, and sent her away.
GENESIS 21:14, NASB

*H*agar moved numbly forward, not knowing where she was going. Left to her own devices, she would have crumbled to the ground and huddled in a fetal position to ward off the waves of grief that overwhelmed her. But for her son's sake, she stood upright.

Never had she imagined this. Yet here she stood, facing an uncertain future. Life once had seemed so simple but now ... oh, what she would give for one yesterday!

Hagar felt so unprotected, victimized. She had served Abraham's wife faithfully. In her desire to bear a son, Sarah had offered Hagar to Abraham, in hopes that she might bring forth an heir. Sarah had never imagined that what had transpired between her servant and her husband could be more than just a physical act.

And yet, Hagar now knew differently. She was merely a servant, but when Abraham laid with her, something had happened inside her. Something took further root as his son grew within her body. The truth was that Hagar had been joined to him not just physically, but spiritually and emotionally as well.

Sarah sensed this, too, and treated Hagar harshly. So harshly that Hagar ran away. But the angel of the Lord had bid her to return. And return she did, until Sarah could bear the sight of Hagar no longer. Abraham had looked apologetic as he sent

Hagar and their son away, but he was determined to keep the peace in his home. Peace at any price.

The ache within Hagar grew as she watched Abraham walk back toward his home, shoulders bent, weary from the bickering of the two women who contended for his love. Hagar knew she was not entitled to his heart. And yet, the fruit of their time together had wrapped its arms around her, tugging her back to present reality. She would never be able to call the love of Abraham her own, and but the ever-present reminder of their union was manifested in the life of her son Ishmael.

She treasured this bittersweet gift; it was all she had left to comfort herself, the sole reminder of a season when she felt loved. No matter how brief the moment, it would have to be enough....

❦

No matter how short the encounter, the act of giving yourself to another plants seeds within the soil of your heart, seeds that bear lasting fruit. You can be sure that every relationship leaves a permanent mark upon our spirits. Long after their departure, the evidence of their presence remains.

Dealing with the residue of past relationships can be an overwhelming proposition. How do you break free from the constant reminders of that lost love? How do you come to terms with the injustice of being cast away in spite of all you have to offer? And worst of all, how do you deal with having to hurt alone when life seems to go on without a ripple for the one who left you weeping in rejection's wake?

Even through the pain of being rejected, we can take comfort knowing that God is near to us, and is well able to turn the bitter to sweet if we embrace his counsel. For he uses every experience to perfect us into greater vessels bearing fruit for his glory.

22

Dear Heavenly Father, I have been the victim of bad choices. Some deliberate, some against my better judgment. I have failed myself and failed you. I admit that I was not prepared for the consequences of my actions, and the burden of them seems too much to bear. So here I stand, looking to your hands for healing. For support and help. Whom have I in heaven but you? Whom have I in the earth besides you?

After all is said and done, you alone are the only one who will not spurn my offerings of love. Forgive me for taking so long to see this. But now I come, mistakes in hand, asking you to take what the enemy meant for evil and make it good. Redeem my past failings and pain and grant me a new beginning. Give me a reason to live and love again. As I embrace you, fill the spaces left behind by those who rejected me, and set me apart for your purposes, to the praise and glory of your name, in Jesus' name. Amen.

– 3 –
Paralysis

*But Lot's wife **looked back** and she became a pillar of salt.*

Genesis 19:26

I knew it," she muttered under her breath. Why should she have expected anything different? This was the story of her life, one upheaval after the other. Every time she hoped things would be different, and every time the taste of disappointment grew more bitter in her mouth. Her comments had long been ignored, so now she went silently.

Lot was a man on the move, and where he went she must follow. Never mind that he never seemed sure where they were going. This was the sacrifice a wife was expected to make for her restless husband. Was it restlessness or a thirst for something else, something more? She could not imagine what that something else might be. All she longed for was the comfort of a permanent place they could call their own. A place to rest her heart, so weary was she from wandering to and fro.

First they had traveled with Abram, who also seemed to follow some invisible voice. Sarah seemed more at peace with his ramblings than she with Lot's. However, she drew comfort from the companionship of another woman in her same situation. But this had changed as the two men with their burgeoning flocks and possessions had outgrown one another and found that parting ways was the only way to a peaceful resolution. So Abram and Sarah had moved on to establish their own way, and Lot's wife felt as though she had left a piece of her heart behind.

Accepting the present, Lot's wife had adjusted and made her new surroundings home, praying that at last her soul could grow roots in this place. But her security was short-lived as they became caught in the crossfire of tribal war. As the kings of Sodom, Gomorrah, Zeboiim, and Zoar fled in defeat, Lot with his family and belongings were kidnapped, spirited away by the enemy. Thank God that Abram had come to the rescue and delivered them safely back to their door, shaken but intact.

And now this. The strangers were telling them that once again Lot and his family must leave. Leave and go where? Everything within her was worn thin from starting over time and time again. Of breaking with the familiar and embracing the new. Growing used to the foreign smells and the sounds all over again. She simply could not start afresh one more time. In her heart she felt like an infant being dragged from the comforting arms of its mother. Her intellect understood that it was not safe for her to remain in her present situation, but the fear of the unknown caused her to distrust her future as well. If it would be more of the same, perhaps she should cut her losses and remain.

But God's grace was greater than her indecision. As she grappled within her spirit to be obedient and flee, the men the Lord had sent hustled her beyond the boundaries of Sodom. Knowing she had mercifully escaped disaster did not comfort her in the early moments of her deliverance. Against God's warning, she turned looking for some sign, some small remembrance that could soothe her torn spirit. And in the turning, her heart slipped from God's safekeeping forever, becoming lost in her yesterdays and former regrets.

As we read in the book of Proverbs, "hope deferred makes the heart sick" (13:12). Disappointment after disappointment may lead us to conclude that perhaps there is nothing better to hope for. Rehearsing the events of the past paralyzes us from moving into the future. It hinders us from daring to hope again.

If our love relationship with God is not the port in which we anchor our hearts, we may become tempted to cling to false harbors that leave our spirits shipwrecked. We sink to the bottom of our own hopelessness and become ensnared in weeds of bitterness. These weeds anchor our souls to the lies of the enemy and kill our spirits slowly. They choke us, making us hard. Cold. Unforgiving and unbending.

When God intervenes, gently pulling us from these deceptive places, we tend to see his protection as an interruption of our desires rather than a deliverance for which we should be grateful. Oh, if only we could see past the valley to the mountain where God waits for us to shake off the enemy's embraces. As we see these false havens for what they really are—the enemy's counterfeits—we will be free to move into the reality of God's promises. It is then we will find a safe sanctuary for our hearts.

Dear Heavenly Father, I am worn and weary and fresh out of hope. I have suffered the upheaval of my heart time and time again, and I no longer have the capacity to move on. I am rooted in my pain. I feel unable to forgive, forget, or release my disappointment.

To be perfectly honest, part of me is afraid to trust you with my future. My present circumstances make it difficult for me to trust in your faithfulness. Oh, how I long to have a different confession and conviction. Hear my heart and answer me. Free me from my pain. Renew my faith. Lead my heart back to your arms where it can rest secure. Help me to begin again, in Jesus' name. Amen.

4

Comparison

⟨⟨∞⟩⟩

*And **Leah's** eyes were weak,*
but Rachel was beautiful of form and face.
GENESIS 29:17, NASB

*L*eah tucked her pain behind her heart and moved on. She should have grown used to this by now. But she hadn't. She would never grow used to being displaced by the beauty of her sister, Rachel.

She would watch the eyes of the men who came calling on her father and brothers, how their eyes would look through her and linger on Rachel, full of longing and admiration. Something inside of her longed to scream, "There's more to me than meets the eye, you know! There is a real woman in here. One who is tender and loving and has a lot to give to a man." But she held her peace. If men were drawn to Rachel's visible qualities over Leah's inner beauty, who was she to judge?

This had been her chance. Her one chance for love. So caught up was she in hoping for a miracle, someone loving her just for her, that Leah never stopped to think of the awful consequences of her father's manipulation.

Laban had cleverly arranged that it was Leah whom Jacob would find on his wedding night. Leah instead of Rachel. So caught up was she that she was ill prepared for Jacob's anger when he discovered the deception the next morning. Nor was she prepared for his determination still to have Rachel by his side. Even if it meant that he would have to work an additional seven years for her father.

Leah wondered at Jacob's love for her sister. After all, in her eyes, Rachel was spoiled and manipulative. But these were things that Jacob could not see, as he toiled for her hand, so blinded was he with adoration. Fourteen years in all. No one had ever wanted Leah enough to go to such lengths to be with her. She wondered how it felt to be loved like that. A piece of Leah died every time she saw the way Jacob looked at Rachel, the way he touched her, the way any little thing she did brought him delight. Leah bent over backward for just a tiny token of affection from him. Her gift was never met with the response that she was seeking. Though she bore him no children, Rachel was still the apple of his eye. Leah bore him son after son, but each new child only heightened her despair. Jacob's love was beyond her reach, entangled in the beauty of Rachel....

The temptation to grow bitter over our own shortcomings looms ever present when we compare ourselves to others. This tendency short-circuits our ability to love our neighbor as we love ourselves.

As the flow of love from our own hearts is hindered by our own insecurities, room is left for others to magnify our imperfections. Failing to see the beauty in ourselves, we fall prey to the empty criticisms of the enemy. We will always be too tall, too short, too fat, too thin, too something if our estimation is based on those around us.

Though we all long to be loved for simply who we are, the love we seek must first be found at the foot of the cross. It is in the light of God's love that we are made whole and lovely. This is a beauty based not on outward packaging, but on the eternal attributes God has placed within us. As we learn to celebrate who we are and bask in his affections, the beauty that radiates from us will draw others to admire the gift that we are to the world.

Dear Heavenly Father, for so long I have labored with the pain of not being enough of whatever others were looking for. I feel so unlovely and unlovable. It seems that others have only confirmed that I am unacceptable.

Open my eyes, that I might see myself the way that you see me. Heal me inwardly and outwardly. Help me to celebrate who I am right now. Surround me with your love and make me whole. May my eyes ever be on you and not on the lives of others, for you have ordained all our days individually and with varying purposes. As I ponder your Word, let it come alive in me that I am fearfully and wonderfully made, just the way I am, for your glory, and that is good! In Jesus' name, Amen.

5

Shattered Dreams

∞

They put Hamor and his son Shechem to the sword and took
Dinah from Shechem's house and left.

GENESIS 34:26

*D*inah made her way hastily through the streets to meet her friends. It was a day like every other. After facing the uncertainty of her family's city of destination, it was refreshing to settle into her new surroundings and establish a routine of sameness. The only girl among a household of male siblings, Dinah longed for the company of women her age. Though she enjoyed her brothers' banter and steadfast protection, her heart always lifted when she could escape their watch and exercise some independence. Perhaps she should not have wandered off alone, but aren't these thoughts always clearer in hindsight?

She felt his eyes long before she met them. From the time her family had moved to Shechem, settling on land purchased from Hamor, his son Shechem had watched her silently. Dinah had kept her distance, knowing he was not a consideration for her future. These people, though friendly, were different from her family, having different customs and serving different gods. Although she longed to be married, she knew that he would be an unacceptable candidate.

But there was no avoiding him today as he stood boldly before her. Usually quite comfortable in the presence of males, she now found herself at a loss for words, feeling quite discomfited by his intense gaze. In his eyes was reflected not the loving consideration of a brother, but a deeper, darker passion with which she was not familiar.

Her emotions ran the gamut, from anguish as he raped her to unbelief at his attempt to comfort her afterward with words of love. She wept bitterly as she thought of her future, which was now hopelessly ruined forever. All that was ahead of her now were years of living alone and in disgrace. She was now unworthy of marriage, having been robbed of the most precious part of her dowry—her virginity. She fought off the waves of despair that threatened to consume her. But Shechem claimed he loved her, and sought to redeem what could have been construed as a tragic event.

His father in tow, Shechem asked Dinah's father, Jacob, for her hand in marriage. She marveled at the calm reaction of her brothers as they set about creating the terms of agreement for their union. All the men of the region would be circumcised, making them acceptable for intermarrying with Jacob's people. Later as Dinah made the journey to Shechem's house, she wondered why she felt so unsettled. The looks in her brothers' eyes did not match their smiles as they shook hands with Shechem and his father. What could they be up to? She soon found out.

As all the men of the city of Shechem recuperated from the agreed-upon circumcision, chaos broke out. Her brothers arrived, killing, pillaging, and looting those now unable to defend themselves. Her cries of protest were ignored as with deadly vengeance they killed her new husband and father-in-law and carried her away, back to her father's house. Dinah numbly moved through the flurry of activity that ensued as they hastily packed and fled to avoid certain retaliation.

How could things have gone so wrong? This was not the life Dinah had planned for herself. She pinched herself to awake, from this horrid dream, but as her tears blurred the road before her, she realized she was indeed awake. Her life would become as endlessly dry and desolate as the scenery that stretched like a long yawn before her. Her brothers seemed self-satisfied that their honor was now intact, won by their act of revenge. But honor meant nothing to her. Honor could not repair an innocent girl's shattered dreams of fulfilled womanhood....

Sometimes life doesn't happen the way that we have imagined it. Things reel out of control. Surprise twists and turns in the journey of life cause us to feel violated, robbed of our own good intentions. Our chance at love is snatched prematurely from our hands, due either to our own choices—or someone else's.

Regret can leave us despairing, stripped of our joy and our peace, feeling unending despondency. Hopes for a better tomorrow are wrenched from our hearts as others rationalize why we should be able to move on. Those responsible for our paralysis continue on without a backward glance, never realizing the depths of the pain they've caused.

Matters of the heart cannot be compartmentalized or tucked into neat little theories. The heart, shaped in the image of the One who loves us most, feels what it feels in spite of itself and forces us to reconcile our longings by placing them in the hands of the only One who can redeem them.

Dear Heavenly Father, somehow my life has gotten beyond my reach, and my dreams have been scattered to the wind. I despair over the lost pieces of my heart. I struggle to repair my shattered spirit. There are so many fragments, some too small to find. It seems impossible to put it all back together.

I need your help. I am confused by the voices of others. I struggle to hear you as I am being pulled between the opposing counsel of my own heart and the well-meaning advice of the loved ones who surround me. My pain overwhelms me.

Who could really know the extent of my suffering? Who can read between the lines of my tears and answer me? Only you. And so with heavy hands I bring all the broken pieces of my heart to you and lay them at your feet, awaiting your restoration. Grant me your peace, restore my joy and make me whole again, in Jesus' name. Amen.

6

*B*etrayal

*So when the Midianite merchants came by, his brothers
pulled **Joseph** up out of the cistern and sold him for twenty shekels
of silver to the Ishmaelites, who took him to Egypt.*

GENESIS 37:28

*J*oseph looked up into the blackness of the night, trying to
find the face of God. His family seemed as far away as the
stars. His own brothers had sold him into slavery. The overwhelming reality was beginning to penetrate his unbelief like
the sting of a resounding slap, not felt immediately, but increasing in pain as each moment passed.

Yes, he was truly in Egypt. He had not felt the earth beneath
his feet as he trudged from his homeland to this foreign place,
so numb was he after being roughly grasped and hustled onward
by the slave traders.

As Joseph was examined by curious eyes and priced like a
common piece of livestock, he thought of the slaves in his
father's house. Had they resented him and his family? Did they
secretly long for freedom? Did they feel shame at their circumstances? This was something he had not thought of before.

All work is honorable, Joseph concluded. The dishonor lies
only in how one achieves his state in life. Joseph's brothers, who
were bound by blood to love and protect him, had betrayed him.
Driven by his father's favoritism and their own jealousy of
Joseph's dreams and aspirations, they sought to rob him of his
own confidence and esteem by interrupting his destiny.

The hours turned to days, the days to years, as Joseph consciously chose to maintain his integrity and faith in spite of what looked like unreasonable circumstances. How could his own brothers have done this to him? Would they get away with it? Would God actually allow them to go skipping merrily into the sunset without an afterthought? Without any sort of sorrow or punishment? Surely God would intervene, and Joseph would have the satisfaction of seeing them gain their comeuppance. In the meantime, he would continue on as best he could.

Joseph rose to prominence in Potiphar's household, only to plummet further into the depths of humiliation at the hands of his master's wife. Yet another who had betrayed him for a selfish motive. Once again Joseph was haunted by the memory of those whose treachery had put him in this position in the first place. They were supposed to have loved him. Supposed to have nurtured and encouraged him, and yet they had not.

If he couldn't trust those who were closest to him, whom could he ever trust in life? What had he done to deserve this wrongful treatment? When would the cycle stop? What was wrong with him? Was there something about himself of which he was unaware that invited these sort of circumstances into his life? He had the answers to none of these questions, therefore he could only turn to the One who did, for it was God and God alone who was able to make one fruitful in the place of one's affliction.

Nothing hurts more than the betrayal of your closest loved ones. Whether it is a family member or a committed love partner, the damage can be deep and extensive. Whether the offense is an act of jealousy, adultery, inconsideration, or thoughtlessness, our hearts are left bleeding. The sting of our suffering, as sharp and sudden as a paper cut, causes us to squeeze the place of our pain and pray for the throbbing to stop.

But the more we press, the deeper the ache goes. We can become slaves to our pain. Toiling to understand the mystery of another person's motives only sets us up for greater bondage. There are no answers in that respect until God chooses to reveal them. Yet as we turn to deal with our own hearts, God meets us with answers and restores us personally if we allow him to touch our wounds.

As we draw close to him, we are able to let go of those who assaulted our hearts to make room for the healing he wants to place in our hands. He alone can cause us to forget our troubles, release the unfinished sentences into his care and embrace new beginnings.

Heavenly Father, I don't understand why I have been treated this way. I have so many unanswered questions. Why did this happen? The pain of rejection and betrayal is overwhelming, and the motives of those who have afflicted me are unclear. When will your vengeance visit those who have rendered this offense against me? When will you right my situation?

I hold your promises of restoration close while I wait for your deliverance. Draw close to me and give me the comfort I seek. Grant me the peace that seems to escape me now. Please, Lord, apply your healing balm of Gilead to my wounds and make me whole once again, in Jesus' name. Amen.

There are so many things I never cried about
dusty painful memories
    I tucked away in a dark drawer
        that I hoped would disappear
        but the moths didn't move fast enough …
and even though they've been ignored
      nevertheless they're there …
      and all the tears I've never cried before
        are now a cold and silent cube of resolve …
   of never again …
and if it melted I could probably
take a long luxurious bath in it
   and emerge quite refreshed and ready
      to slip into loving you …
        but I'm not sure
          that all the pain
            can ever dry
and how can I know that you won't add
   another drop
      to all the tears
        I've never cried before ….

$\mathcal{F}$alse Intimacy

∽◌∽

But Onan knew that the offspring would not be his;
so whenever he lay with his brother's wife, he spilled his seed
on the ground to keep from producing offspring for his brother.
GENESIS 38:9

$\mathcal{T}$amar lay perfectly still, watching Onan's face as he with-
drew himself. Did he think she was a fool, unaware of
what he was doing? At first she had blamed herself every time
her menstrual cycle started. Perhaps she was defective, unable to
bear children. The possibility of disgrace and the prospect of
never holding her own child in her arms pierced her heart and
increased her mourning.

When she was given in marriage to Er, the son of Judah, life
had seemed so promising. He had come from an elite and influ-
ential family. But alas, Er was also wicked. So wicked that the
Lord had put him to death. Now, according to God's law, Onan
was to take her as his wife and produce a child to continue his
brother's lineage.

But Onan was not interested in splitting what he had with a
son that would not be considered his. However, he would not
refuse the selfish pleasure of sleeping with Tamar. And so he
spilled his seed on the ground.

In time Tamar realized that the fault lay not with her. Onan
was taking advantage of her situation. But where could she turn,
whom could she tell? Who would come to her defense? No one,
or so she thought.

God saw the wicked behavior of Onan. His transgression was

not only against Tamar but against God's law. So God took Onan's life, too.

Tamar could not decide if her tears were over Onan's death or over her last immediate chance to conceive. She wondered at the awful games life was playing on her. Why did her fate always lie in the hands of men? They could be so cruel. After all, she wanted so little. Just someone to love ... and to be loved in return.

❦

Intimacy without responsibility always leads to heartbreak. Someone always gets hurt. It can be devastating to give your all to a relationship, only to discover that you are on the path to nowhere. While some willfully endanger a meaningful relationship by ignoring the word of God and partaking in sex before marriage, just as many take the right path and find themselves victims of their own sincerity and honest effort.

Many a misleading relationship has been wrapped in the guise of "friendship." Guard your heart when someone says, "Let's just be friends," but continues to make intimate overtures in conversation and gestures that make you hope for more. Dangling the inviting carrots of a promising relationship before you, he makes a commitment to someone else, then absolves himself of blame by reminding you, "I said we were just friends."

It is no wonder you are hurting. This man has spilled the seeds of his heart on the ground before you. He has withheld his love, leaving you to feel spurned, rejected, and betrayed. Instead of being outraged by his dishonesty and insensitivity, you may begin to question your own worth: What's wrong with me? What did I do wrong? Why wasn't my love returned?

Pain. Shame. Hopelessness. These are the emotions that haunt every unfruitful relationship. If allowed to roost they bear the fruit of bitterness. "The next man will have a hard way to go," becomes the unspoken vow of the heart that has lost the ability to trust. Little do men who abuse hearts in the name of "friendship" realize they have indeed affected the inheritance of their "brothers."

On the other hand, we must be careful never to "roll over" a debt of unforgiveness. The next prospect for love is not responsible for what has transpired before. Every disappointment must be buried at the foot of the cross, so that we might recognize true love when it comes and embrace it without reserve.

Dear Heavenly Father, how could I have been so foolish? I thought he really loved me, and that I only had to give him the time to see his own heart. But somewhere along the way I missed all the cues, so blinded was I by my own desires. And now the pain is more than I can bear.

I am not sure which hurts the most—my heart or my self-esteem. Will I ever find a man to love me the way I long to be loved? And how can I face those around me who watched me give my all? Their sympathy is almost as painful as the rejection, so deep is my shame.

Forgive me for releasing my heart to one who was undeserving. Help me to give my heart to you with the same abandon with which I have given it to others. I never seem to appreciate your love until my heart has been abandoned by others. For this I am deeply sorry. Help me to release this offense and to begin again in you, safe and warm, fruitful once again in your love. In Jesus' name. Amen.

$\mathcal{B}$roken Promises

*When Judah saw her, he thought she was a **prostitute**,*
for she had covered her face.
GENESIS 38:15

"$\mathcal{W}$ell, a woman's got to do what a woman's got to do," Tamar thought to herself as she adjusted her veil and waited by the side of the road. She had been the victim of so many broken promises, now she was determined to take her destiny into her own hands, by hook or by crook.

When Er died, Tamar had comforted herself with the fact that Onan would take her as his wife and sire an heir to continue her husband's name according to their custom and law. Then her hopes were once again snuffed out, first by his disobedience to God's law, then by Onan's premature death.

She made the trek back to her father's house to live as a widow until Judah's third son, Shelah, was old enough to carry out this family duty. As she went, she didn't know which was heavier, her empty arms or her grieving heart. Tamar had no husband and no child. None of the things that gave a woman validation and security.

Year after year passed. Too many years. Surely Judah should have summoned her. Shelah was certainly old enough by now to do right by her. Still, no word came. Judah had blamed Tamar for the loss of his first two sons; he was afraid of losing another in her arms.

So here she sat, disguised as a prostitute, waiting for her father-in-law to come her way. This time she would not accept a mere promise from him. She would make him fulfill it.

Judah, whose wife had died, saw Tamar by the side of the road and propositioned her. As he had his way with her and satisfied himself, Tamar merely went through the motions, keeping her mind fixed on securing her own desire—a child. She had been used before, now she would become the user. As she made her way home with his staff and the seal he had given her as a down payment for her "services," she prayed that his seed would take root within her.

In time Tamar grew swollen with child, and rumors began to swirl around her. Not knowing of Tamar's ruse, everyone assumed the worst, and word reached Judah that Tamar had been guilty of prostitution. Judah ordered her to be brought out and burned to death. In response she sent his seal and staff, with a message: "I am pregnant by the man who owns these."

With this revelation Judah's wrath was stayed and his shame became her covering. Whatever the fabric, the garment was fine with her. Cradling her twins in her arms, Tamar again sighed, "A woman's got to do what a woman's got to do."

❦

Broken promises and a string of unfruitful relationships can birth deception in the heart of a woman, a deception so subtle it may be hard for her to perceive it. The idea that men cannot be trusted has caused many women to cloak their hearts in garments they would not usually wear, and to conclude that men can be relied upon only as a means of sexual and financial fulfillment.

Those who have been hurt may be tempted to hurt others in a similar fashion, not out of revenge but out of fear. The temptation takes many forms: extracting commitment from one who is unwilling to give it freely. Extricating validation at another's expense for your own personal satisfaction. Soliciting love with no thought of returning it. Protecting your heart, even from the person who has let you inside his.

To give yourself without sincerity in order to reach another goal—be it financial, physical, or emotional—is a form of prostitution. It will always leave you feeling used, disappointed in yourself, and doubtful of God's willingness to provide for you.

Such actions rob you of your ability to be transparent with others. Those around you may not know the details of your past pain, but they sense the deception. And the barrier between you and those who can give you the love you seek grows higher and higher. Though your heart is protected, you are left imprisoned, harboring empty prizes and wondering why a better tomorrow never comes.

It is only the heart that remains open, that dares to hope again, that finds a safe refuge in the fullness of God's timing. As we come out of denial and embrace our pain, knowing that it whispers answers to our questions and gives us the clues we need to get to the other side of our fears, our cumulative experiences birth a hope that will never make us ashamed.

Dear Heavenly Father, I have grown bitter and hopeless. I must admit that the repeated cycle of disappointments in my life has made me into someone that I really am not. I long to start over, but I'm afraid. Afraid to trust. To hope. To love again. To trust you for a different ending to my next love story. I'm afraid to wait on you because I feel that even you have disappointed me. And so I have chosen to take my heart out of your hands and protect it myself. But in dressing it to keep out the chill of rejection, I have insulated it from all the good things you have in store for me as well.

Help me. Help me to open my hands and take you at your word. Help me to trust you, to release my heart back into your care and to realize your promises as reality. As I limp back to your arms, cover me in the garments of vulnerability and hope. I know this is the only way to receive from you and I long to be blessed. Keep my heart and make it beat with a faith in love once again, in Jesus' name. Amen.

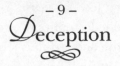Deception

*The men of Israel **sampled** their **provisions***
but did not inquire of the Lord.
JOSHUA 9:14

They stood off in the distance, clocking the movements of the Israelites, learning their routine, absorbing any and all information that would be helpful. The more they knew about these people, the better to gain their confidence.

From the time the news had spread through the region that the Israelites were headed their way, claiming territory and wiping out their enemies as they went, the Gibeonites had begun devising a way to win them over. If they could get the Israelites to sign a treaty with them, their lives would be secure.

The Gibeonites knew that the Israelites were not always disagreeable to foreigners. Why, they even had Egyptians among them! The same people that had kept them in bondage for years. Obviously they were a forgiving people. Either that, or they were complete fools.

Adjusting their garments and adding another layer of dust to everything they carried for more effect, they rehearsed their story one last time. They rearranged the cracked wine skins and moldy bread they carried, more out of nervous energy than anything else, and started out. Affecting a look of weariness, they made their way to the center of the Israelite camp in search of Joshua.

When they found the leader of the Israelites, the Gibeonites pleaded their case with him, saying that they had come from a long way to make league with them. They dared not breathe easily until they had gained Joshua's trust. As he questioned them, they revealed their spoiled supplies to prove how they had suffered the rigors of a long and arduous journey. All of their provisions had been brought fresh from home—now look at them!

They waited silently, trembling inwardly as the Israelites carefully examined everything and counseled among themselves. Then they sighed with relief when Joshua finally agreed to enter into covenant with them.

Their relief was interrupted by panic three days later, when the Israelites uncovered their ruse. What would be their fate?

After reprimanding them for their deception, the irate Joshua said only that they would be cursed with servitude for the rest of their days. The strange God the Israelites served took vows very seriously, and though the Gibeonites were enemies, the Israelites were bound by the oath they had made.

Servants? Again the imposters felt a rush of relief. They were happy to be servants. Bondage was better than death.

◈

So often women enter into love covenants with those who come disguised as Mr. Right. Like the men of Israel who never took the time to look beyond the surface, some women hear words and romantic gestures and take them at face value, without inquiring of the Lord.

Because of the covenant made with the Gibeonites, the Israelites were pulled into an unnecessary war to protect the land that their "enemy" inhabited. Years later, the Israelites suffered a three-year famine because of the zeal of Saul, King of Israel, who ignored the covenant and sought to wipe the Gibeonites out of the land. All of this needless difficulty was a result of a moment's thoughtless impulse.

Oh, the pain of discovering that the person you placed your trust in is not who he pretended to be! And oh, the shame of knowing you have no one to blame but yourself! Perhaps the Holy Spirit whispered to you that this man was not "the one," but the need of your heart drowned out that still, small voice.

Perhaps you heard nothing and chose to trust your own instincts. He said all the right things. His actions were consistent in the beginning, so that your heart felt safe in this person's hands. And now you find yourself enslaved by your own misperceptions. His true colors came out in time, but by then you were in too deep! Too deep to extricate your heart without experiencing pain.

Once again your hopes are dashed. "True love"—or, at least, one who appeared to be loving—turned out to be nothing more than a counterfeit. Can you ever trust your own judgment or discernment again? If actions are all you have to go by, how will you know when you have truly met the one that God has intended for you?

Only by committing your heart to God, who is able to keep it safe.

Our need for love can get us into trouble if we leave our hearts uncovered as we travel toward the promise. This is why 2 Timothy warns that "there will be terrible times in the last days. People will be lovers of themselves, lovers of money, boastful, proud, abusive, disobedient to their parents, ungrateful, unholy, without love, unforgiving, slanderous, without self-control, brutal, not lovers of the good, treacherous, rash, conceited, lovers of pleasure rather than lovers of God—having a form of godliness but denying its power. Have nothing to do with them. They are the kind who worm their way into homes and gain control over weak-willed women, who are loaded down with sins and are swayed by all kinds of evil desires, always learning but never able to acknowledge the truth" (3:1-7).

Though the desire for love is not inherently evil, it leaves us open to deception and sin if our desires are not left at the foot of the cross, awaiting God's perfect timing for fulfillment. If our desire for anyone or anything is a higher priority than our desire for God, we become vulnerable to the manipulation of those who don't always have the best of intentions. Like Joshua, we must forgive and release those who have deceived us into the hands of God (or enter into the bondage of bitterness ourselves).

Trust God to redeem your mistakes. He is able to make all things beautiful in time, though the journey to peace might be a difficult one—and one that could have been avoided.

Remember, God doesn't waste anyone's time. If you are willing to place your mistakes on the altar, he will continue to work in your life to bring about rich rewards, lessons that you might not have learned any other way.

Dear Heavenly Father, my heart is still stinging from the deception I have experienced. I feel so foolish. My need for love drowned out your instructions and I gave my heart to an unworthy stranger. And though I now see the truth about this person, I'm finding it difficult to sever this relationship. My soul is tied to his and I can't find a way to disconnect, even though I know this man is not your will for my life.

I long so deeply for someone to love me that I settled for crumbs instead of the banquet you were preparing. My pride has been assaulted, and my spirit torn because of my own shortsightedness. I was too busy grasping at what I wanted to ask you what you wanted.

Help me to forgive myself, and to reclaim the peace I can only find in you. Touch my heart. Heal my wounds. Restore my faith. Help me to learn from this and move on, trusting you for a new beginning, in Jesus' name. Amen.

Love does not lose, you forfeit.
And the pain that erodes comes not from the loss
but from the bitterness that detains you
from loving again.

C.J. Wilson in _Limited Vision_

*U*ncovering

∞

*When he reached home, he took a knife and cut up his **concubine**,*
limb by limb, into twelve parts and sent them into
all the areas of Israel.

JUDGES 19:29

Though she understood her father had no choice but to
sell her as a concubine, she was afraid she could no
longer keep her end of the bargain. As she walked the weari-
some journey back to her family home, she concluded that she
preferred to be unmarried rather than submit herself to being
in a household that was not really her own. To have the duties
but not the privilege or status of a wife was something she could
not abide. Especially to a man who made her life unbearable.
The members of his household made her days even darker.

No one dared to speak against the "man of God" simply
because he bore the title of a Levite. They were such a legalistic,
religious, condescending group. They saw how she was being
treated, yet they said nothing. *She should grin and bear it,* was their
sentiment. *That is what God requires of a woman.* About this she
had her doubts.

She felt she had reclaimed her peace as she settled into life at
home. She would learn to live with the disapproving stares and
whispers of those around her. At least she was her own woman
once again.

Her comfort was short-lived. After several months her peace
was shattered by the unwelcome figure of her husband coming
around the bend to reclaim her. She fought down her panic,

steeling herself inwardly. Death would be better than returning with him. She dared not trust his unfamiliar kind words as he entreated her to return home with him. Out of paternal pity her father cajoled her husband into staying a few days longer. But five days of grace were all that she was given. Her husband finally insisted that they return home, and her father was powerless to detain them any longer.

They made their way in silence traveling through Benjamite territory, each step causing the burden of her heart to grow beyond her ability to bear it. She would welcome sleep this night. As they sat waiting for someone to offer them hospitality in the unfamiliar town square, she wondered at the fate of her tomorrows. She was at the mercy of this man who gave her no reason to look forward to another day.

The kind face of one stranger offering them hospitality brought momentary relief; something about the manner of the others passing by had caused her to shiver in trepidation. As they made their way to his home, again she thought of how much she longed to escape her present reality, if only for a few hours, in her dreams. But then the night turned more terrifying than anything she had experienced in all her days.

Loud banging and raucous voices interrupted the pleasantness of their temporary sanctuary. Men at the door demanded that her husband be turned over to them. They wanted to have sex with him! Their host looked deeply ashamed, yet determined to protect his guest. Speaking peacefully to them availed nothing. When the men adamantly refused to go away, the host in desperation offered them his virgin daughter and … her! She couldn't have heard him correctly … and yet it was true.

She stood rooted to the spot, paralyzed by disbelief. Through her haze of terror she heard the high-pitched, desperate weeping of the young girl who pleaded with her father and clung to him in fear. Out of the corner of her eye, she saw her husband hastily grasp her arm. She felt as if she was outside of her body as she sensed that she was being roughly led toward the door. As it slammed behind her, she found herself gazing into the hostile, wanton eyes of strange men. Dragged and mishandled, stripped and molested over and over again, she prayed for the nightmare to end.

Suddenly the silence around her was deafening. The sun rose in the sky, slowly, as if embarrassed to illuminate her shame. She made her way back to the stranger's house where her husband lay sleeping, gritting her teeth against the pain she felt from the tips of her toes to her scalp. Through the haze of anguish that racked her entire being she fought to return, not really knowing why. Why return to a place that held no comfort? No protection. Why go back to a man who could only offer her more of the same? He did not love her. Did not cover her.

Yet it was all she knew. There was nowhere else for her to go.

Resigning herself to the blackness that engulfed her, she lay at the door with no strength left to knock. She wept over her nakedness, over her shame, over the lack of all she craved.... *So life has come to this,* she thought, and died.

She did not feel her husband nudge her unfeelingly, for she was beyond feeling. Neither did she hear him say, "Let's be on our way," for she was beyond hearing harsh words. She did not feel him put her on his donkey or feel the bumpy journey home; she was beyond caring where and how she went.

She did not feel him cutting her body into pieces. She was beyond wincing from cruelty any longer. She did not witness the outrage of the men who gathered from every region to decry how such a horrible thing could have been done. It no longer mattered; their defense of her plight came too late. She would never know that at last her honor was avenged as they made war against the tribe of Benjamin, destroying their cities and killing their wives and children. She was beyond believing that anyone cared. She did not witness the distress of the Benjamite men who were left without wives, now facing the extinction of their tribe, because of the ravages of war. She was beyond feeling the torment of lack. Yes, she was finally beyond it.

❦

Something happens when a man does not cover a woman. It may be her father who does not protect her. Or it could be her husband who does not live up to the call of a godly bridegroom, refusing to give his life for his wife. Either way, she is stripped naked, defenseless, and open to violation.

The world has rough hands that can strip a woman's emotions, bruise her heart, wound her body, damage her psyche, and tear her spirit asunder. And though we struggle to find our original selves—full of hope and the possibilities of love, the lack of affirmation from the men in our lives can make us die inside quietly, unable to feel, to respond, to even voice our pain. The shattered pieces of our hearts are scattered abroad upon the winds of lovelessness.

It is in this painful place that the determinations of the heart must be settled. God is the only perfect father, the only bridegroom who gives his all—his love, his protection, his comfort, unconditionally. It is only as we cover ourselves in the blood of Jesus that we can hope again. As we abide under the shadow of the Almighty, it is in the secret place that we find the protection our hearts seek and the healing our spirits crave.

Dear Heavenly Father, the one that I trusted to protect me has betrayed me. I have nowhere to go. No one is coming to my defense. My emotions overwhelm me—fear, anger, anguish, the desire for retaliation. It seems too much to bear. I pray for relief. Then the numbness comes, and I wish I could feel again.

I'm so alone, Lord. When will I feel whole again? Feel loved again? Feel joy again? Where are you, Lord? I thought that you loved me and yet I feel abandoned even by you. When will you show yourself strong on my behalf?

I need your covering. I need your help. If you are really there, hearken unto my cry and deliver me from the pain and shame. I feel so unworthy. So abused.

Touch me, Lord, bind me up, strengthen me, and lift me from this place. Help me find the shattered pieces of my heart. You are my only hope. Let me experience the abundant life Jesus died to give me. I have wept through the night; give me the joy that is promised in the morning. Take my hand, show me the way to healing, and grant me a new beginning. In Jesus' name. Amen.

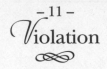Violation

Her brother Absalom said to her, "Has that Amnon,
your brother, been with you? Be quiet now, my sister;
he is your brother. Don't take this thing to heart."
And Tamar lived in her brother Absalom's house,
a desolate woman.

2 SAMUEL 13:20

Her weeping came from the depths of her soul and rang through the canyons of her entire being. Clutching her torn garments to her breast as if to reserve the last shreds of her dignity, she made her way across the courtyard. The ashes with which she had covered herself were a silent witness to the stain of a violation no tears could wash away. Nothing could. If she took a thousand baths, she would still feel unclean.

She was empty, spent, a prisoner of her own despair. Tamar could still feel Amnon's eyes glaring at her with intense hatred. Still hear his words ringing in her ears, "Get this woman out of here and bolt the door behind her." This woman! *This woman!* She had been deceived and raped, but being reduced to just another woman in her brother's eyes was more than she could bear.

The sounds of her suffering carried on the wind, drawing the attention of her brother Absalom. He came bounding from his house to see what had so devastated her.

She felt so ashamed as she shared her plight with him. Would he blame her for this? Would he say that she had done something to entice Amnon? The thought of his name caused her to shiver in repulsion. She thought her stepbrother liked her. She had caught his gaze many times when he did not avert his eyes quickly enough to conceal his longing. It was inconceivable that he had such evil intentions toward her. Though they did not share the same mother, the blood of their father David joined them together in a familial bond that could not be ignored.

She had been summoned to cook for Amnon because he was ill. It never occurred to her that he would force himself upon her. It was unnecessary. If his desire for her was that great, all he had to do was speak to their father and ask for permission to marry her. Instead he stripped her of her garments, ignoring her pleas. Stripped her of her virginity. Stripped her of her dignity. Stripped her of any hope of ever being married.

Now it was too late. The moment he was finished having his way with her, Amnon's "love" changed to hatred. As a matter of fact, he hated her more now than he had ever loved her. Now he cast her aside carelessly, as if he had never known her at all.

Now where could she turn? Who would come to her defense? No one had been present to hear her cries, to witness this travesty. Absalom could only clumsily comfort her by suggesting that she should not take this matter to heart. Though Absalom did not accuse her, his attempts to calm her did not repair her shredded soul. How could she not take it to heart? The inner core of her being had been brutally invaded. Her very soul had been ravaged and left for dead.

Yes, a part of her had died that day. It did not come back to life when, after several years, Absalom avenged her by killing Amnon. His death could not console her devastated heart. And as she wandered the halls of Absalom's house, day in and day out, she resigned herself to believing that only the night and her dreams would give her relief from the desolation that had taken up residence within her.

CR

All men are mandated by God to treat the women in their lives with respect and honor. They are called to protect and cover us, as we are the physically weaker vessels. However, the heart of fallen man does not always heed the call of the Spirit. When flesh rules, men and women alike fall prey to selfishness, impulsiveness, impatience, lust, covetousness, manipulation, strife, and every evil work.

The cycle of violation that follows sinks the soul into deeper and deeper depravity, wreaking more and more destruction on others not aware of the pain of the offender. Whether it is an abusive mother that builds fury in the heart of a man, or some other past relationship or painful incident, no one knows the motivation of one who violates and damages another person's heart, body, or spirit.

One can be raped emotionally as well as physically. A person's heart can be violated by the misinterpreted or deceptive motives of another. In the mind of the victim, a thousand "whys" remain unanswered. There may never be a visible rhyme or reason behind actions of abuse, rape, betrayal, or adultery. Emotional devastation can go deeper than physical abuse, simply because it can be more difficult to locate the source of suffering in order to deal with it.

Neither party walks away unscathed by these painful encounters. Regardless of what the eyes see, both people pay, both lose pieces of themselves. Both become people with the potential to hurt others over and over again until the root of their anger is dealt with. Such is the cycle of unresolved pain.

And yet, the power of God's healing is always available. If we are to stop the cycle of pain, we must first extricate ourselves in order to embrace the One who comes with healing arms to comfort us. We will never forget the experience, but we must choose to understand (this does not mean justify) and forgive the one who has wronged us. If we allow ourselves to become prisoners of unforgiveness and bitterness, we are sentenced to live a life of seclusion, self-loathing, and hopelessness.

Dear Heavenly Father, what I feel goes so deep within me I do not know how to begin to unravel the mess that is inside of my heart. My confidence has been shattered. I search my heart to see if there is anything in me that invited this violation and I find nothing, yet I feel shame. I feel unclean. I feel totally and completely alone in my pain. No one else could possible know how I feel right now.

Where can I turn but to you? I am so angry and yet I feel defenseless. Powerless to right the wrong that has been done to me or even bring the perpetrator to justice. Who will come to my defense besides you? You are all I have. Yet I am so filled with unforgiveness that I wonder if you will hear me. I need your help. I am so afraid that if I let go of my anger, an even more frightening emotion will engulf me—fear. Fear that it will happen again. Fear that I will completely cave in to my trauma. Fear that the spirit of self-preservation inside of me will wither and die if I allow myself to feel without a buffer.

Help me to let go, to allow you to right this wrong. Help me trust in your justice and to concentrate on the mending of my own spirit.

Comfort and heal me now. Wash my wounds and heal even my scars. And though it is inconceivable in this moment that I will ever feel real joy again, I ask that you would turn my mourning to laughter, my sorrow into praise. And help me to take this experience and use it for your glory and the good of others, in Jesus' name. Amen.

$\mathcal{F}$ruitless Searching

The **watchmen** found me as they made their rounds in the city.
They beat me, they bruised me; they took away my cloak,
those **watchmen** of the walls!
SONG OF SONGS 5:7

$\mathcal{T}$hough it was dark and this was not the best section of town, she pressed forward in search of her lover. Perhaps she should have waited until the morning, but the urgent need of her heart spurred her on as she peered down deserted streets, around dark corners, and inside late-night establishments looking for him. At times she thought she saw him in the distance, but each time she drew close enough to see him, she realized that the familiar shape was that of a stranger. After encountering many that bore a faint resemblance to the one she pursued, she found herself much further than she had planned to venture. The hair on the back of her neck prickled as she sensed that she had wandered beyond the boundaries of safety. But even this did not detain her from continuing on.

She heard them before she saw them. Startled by their voices, she jumped, then drew a breath of relief. It was merely the watchmen. They would know where he was. But before she could utter a word they were upon her. Battering her with questions as they pushed and shoved her. What was she doing out this time of night? Where was she going? What was her manner of business? Only a prostitute would wander in these parts this late in the evening. As they ripped her veil from her face to get a closer look she protested against their assumptions. No! No!

She was none of the things they called her. She was merely a woman in search of love. Was this a crime?

Badly shaken and bruised, she stumbled home, dazed by her fruitless expedition. All she had wanted was to find the one her heart was seeking. For this she should be brutalized and made to feel so cheap? As she crumpled on her bed for another sleepless night, she wondered if her longing for love would ever be realized. Was it just a dream that one had knocked at the door of her heart, called her name, and whispered promises of love? For now she would not know the answer. She dared not venture out again.

❧

Many have found themselves looking for love in all the wrong places and faces. They have been bruised, their actions misinterpreted. They lavished their hearts on someone who responded too slowly or with obscure intentions.

The Shulamite in Song of Songs had missed her lover, responding to his call too late at night. When at last she reconsidered and rose from her bed to meet her husband, he was already gone. Instead she met the harsh indifference of someone who did not love her at all. She returned home "sick with love."

It was true then and is still true now. "*He* who finds a wife finds a good thing and receives favor from the Lord" (Prv 18:22, NASB). Yes, ladies, the *man* was created to pursue. When we move out of place and out of season in search of love, our spirits are wounded needlessly. We are stripped of the covering that God has provided to protect our hearts.

When women become the pursuers, their advances are misinterpreted for desperation or aggression or promiscuity. This opens the door for their hearts to be mishandled even if their advances are returned. You see, only the man that God has chosen to love you will know the deep needs of your heart because he was specially crafted to be your partner in life.

God has placed everything in that man that you need, and vice versa. Moving out of turn, out of spiritual order, brings needless complications, and results in unsatisfying relationships that were never meant to be. The cycle of broken relationships can be debilitating, making the heart sick from hope deferred. If our hearts are broken once too often, it becomes hard to believe the concept that true love will one day be ours.

Ah, but as we draw close to God and place our hearts back into his protective care, he draws close, loving the hurt away and whispering promises of love forever and ever.

Dear Heavenly Father, I admit that I have taken my love life into my own hands and gone in search of love in all the wrong places. Please forgive my impatience. My lack of trust. I have failed to rest in the knowledge that in due season you would bring to me the one that you have appointed. I have tried and tried again to no avail to locate a man that would love me the way I long to be loved. Time and time again I thought I had found him, only to suffer deep disappointment when the love I gave was not returned.

And now I come to you with open hands, holding the remains of my bleeding heart. A heart I should have left in your care in the first place. As I lay it back on your altar, help me to release it without second thoughts. Help me to rest in you, completely relying on your timing and selection. As I look back on all the mistakes I've made, I can see the fruitlessness of my own efforts.

I release my life back into your hands and trust that you will withhold no good thing from me. Yes, I will wait for the good and perfect gift that you have in mind. I yield myself to you now, to make me and mold me into a good thing to present to the man of your choice, that our union may be to the glory of your name and the fulfillment of your kingdom plan, in Jesus' name. Amen.

13

Sorrow of Sorrows

O Jerusalem, Jerusalem … how often I have longed to gather
your children together, as a hen gathers her chicks
under her wings, but you were not willing!

LUKE 13:34

He stood looking over the city with heavy heart. So many people rushing to and fro, and yet he knew the story of each and every one. Little did they know how he longed after them. Prayed for them. Wanted to protect them from the evil one. He had extended kindness after kindness. Performed miracle after miracle. Taught lesson after lesson. And still they did not know his heart toward them.

In his foreknowledge he knew that those who had gathered to hang on his every word would be the same ones who would exchange his life for that of a mere criminal. Those who cried "Hosanna to the Son of David!" would also be the ones who cried, "Crucify him!"

He knew that he would be with them only for a season, already knew the outcome of his mission. Even so, it did not hurt any less, knowing that those he came to save, to pour his love out upon, would reject him. Still he gave freely, driven by his desire and the passion of the Father to restore hearts from their fallen condition. In spite of their rejection, he was willing to give his life for them. He prayed that the Father would keep them until the day of their reckoning. That they would learn to overcome the tests and trials of life. That they would be empowered to be victorious over temptation.

His heart was broken for them, even as his body would soon be broken for them. Perhaps it was because he understood their blindness, their lack of understanding, that he did not relent or turn back from his painful mission. Even after enduring the betrayal of those closest to him. The cowardice of secret admirers. The fickleness of those who had celebrated him. The taunts of the incensed mob. The apathy of those who determined his fate. The humiliation of being beaten, stripped, and crucified. His conclusion was still the same. It didn't matter what they did to him, he loved them just the same.

His heart was not moved by their lack of love or appreciation. He answered a higher call, a call to love unconditionally. In spite of them, he would love. As he hung his head and died, he concluded one thing.

If he had to do it all again, he would.

He was despised and rejected by men, a man of sorrows, and familiar with suffering. Like one from whom men hide their faces he was despised, and we esteemed him not (Is 53:3).

When we are hurting from the pain of love rejected, it is hard to recall a time when we inflicted such suffering on another. And yet at some time in our lives, we have all been guilty of ignoring one who longed after us. Jesus Christ is the only man who perfectly understands love, for he was love in the flesh. That love came and dwelt among us and we with our limited vision did not recognize it.

Who could know more about the pain of being unappreciated by those you love most? He too suffered heartbreak, rejection, abuse, betrayal, loneliness. Even being fatherless. He knows what it feels like to be rejected by the one you poured your heart out to. He's been there and emerged victorious. This is why he is the only one we can bring the shattered pieces of our hearts to. He is the great restorer of broken spirits and tattered souls. He binds up our wounds and makes us whole again with the ointment that was pressed from his own suffering, on our behalf.

Dear Jesus, thank you for giving your life for me. Thank you for loving me when I didn't love you back. Thank you for listening even when I failed to seek you. For coming to my aid when others were more important to me than you were.

Thank you for being faithful to me even when my heart strayed from you in search of other lovers. I am humbled by your consistency, by your willingness to love me in spite of myself. This is the type of love I have been seeking in all the wrong places. Perfect my love for you. Make yourself a reality to me like never before. Open my eyes to see your heart and hear your Holy Spirit.

I now give you my heart willingly, and entrust it into your safekeeping. Come and fill me with your divine love. Teach me to love as you loved. To love you with all my heart, all my soul, and all my strength. To love myself as you made me—good and perfect. To love my neighbor as I love myself. Help me to seek you morning and evening, at every opportunity, for that is what love does. It never stops reaching, is ever seeking the object of its affection. Lord, I choose to begin afresh this day by recommitting my heart to you daily, in Jesus' name. Amen.

The Process

❧

The pain of heartbreak can strike suddenly. It takes only a moment to sever a relationship, betray a trust, dash a hope. It takes much longer to recover from it. There are no magical cures, no quick fixes. The journey toward healing must be made slowly and carefully. We must deal gently with our hearts as layers of the soul heal a day at a time.

The pain, the shock, the numbness, anger, bitterness, and resignation. The full myriad of feelings must be acknowledged and dealt with, one by one, until they are all resolved. How long does it take? Well, that depends on the depth of the wound.

The process of weathering trials, emotional or otherwise, should be embraced. In the process of healing, we uncover secrets to growth and maturity. If we are patient, we will accumulate a wealth of experience that cements our faith and causes us to look confidently toward the future.

To be sure, this is not a pleasant season in anyone's life. However, this too shall pass. And as the storm ceases, the clouds will part to reveal a sun that shines more brilliantly than before. The grass is greener, the sky bluer because everything has been cleansed and refreshed by heaven's tears.

Pain is a necessary part of living. Without it we would have no reference point for joy. Lush valleys abound at the foot of the mountain, watered by the brooks that flow down its sides to the thirsty earth below. This is the cycle of life, the ups and the downs. The dry places, the seasons of watering. The birth of a dream, the death of a vision, the resurrection of a lost hope.

Of one thing you can be sure, whatever is good and perfect will remain and the rest, thankfully, will be removed. It is the letting go that alarms our hearts, for they are creatures of habit, reluctant to change or release that which has been held dear. Yet let go we must, grow we must, move on we must. The one thing we must never do is avoid the process of God's transforming work within us.

Dearest Michelle,

These are reflections of my own life's experiences, things that have helped me come to terms with life's challenges. I hope that they will give you encouragement and lift you up to steer ahead.

An old headmistress of mine always used to say: *"Flatter me and I may not believe you. Criticize me and I may not like you. Ignore me and I may not forgive you. But encourage me and I will never forget you."* The world is not a fair place, and things do not work and happen the way we perceive them or want them to, for our convenience and well-being. Life is made up of ups and downs. But what we have to do is face the reality of the harsh world in which we live and move on.

The most important part of moving on is to forgive—you can't make progress when you are facing the wrong way (which for us may seem to be the right way). Forgive those who hurt you and redirect all the emotional energy you've given to bitterness toward fulfilling your destiny.

Do something every day to change your attitude—instead of trying to think your way into right acting, act your way into right thinking. Act the person you want to be and gradually that's the person you will become.

Only when you learn to accept the person that you are can you accept and enjoy others as they are. A great historian (whose name escapes me and probably wouldn't mean much to you anyway) said, "Your attitude is your best friend or your worst enemy— it will either draw people to you or keep them away. It is never content until it has been expressed, and in every case it is more honest and consistent than your words. It is the librarian of your past, the speaker of your present, and the prophet of your future."

Don't allow yourself to be swept away by the distraction that disappointments can bring. Discover your life's purpose and anchor yourself to it before the bell rings and "class closes."

First – *"Know God."* He alone holds the key to unlock the secret of who we really are.

Second – *"Know yourself."* You can only love what you know and fix what you understand. It is dangerous when others know you better than you know yourself, for knowledge is power. What are your real needs, values, goals, boundaries?

Third – *"Know your neighbor."* We are born alone, die alone, but we are not meant to live alone. We need to love and be loved and that takes time. How can anyone talk to you for twenty minutes and say they know you? They are either brilliant or you are shallow. Knowing someone takes time.

People respond better to kindness than complaints. In fact, most people will do nearly anything if you treat them with kindness. That means making it clear to them that their feelings are important, their preferences respected, and their opinions valuable. It also means giving them the benefit of the doubt. We all make mistakes. Therefore, every man is entitled to be valued by his best moments.

When failure knocks at the door, it is sometimes just a signal that it is time to change direction. If you keep hitting a wall, back up and look for a door. If you take a detour, don't despair, it may be the road that you should have been on in the first place. Failing does not make you a failure, only quitting does. So have faith, step out and DO; if you make mistakes you will be the wiser afterward.

When you don't believe in yourself, you will always expect the worst from others. It is easy to allow our hearts to lie dormant for fear—do not let low self-esteem and the disappointments of the past blind you to the new options that present themselves daily. Dare to try again and trust God to be your safety net. It is the leap of faith that can be both most dangerous, yet most rewarding.

Best regards,
Yvonne

14

*A*cknowledge
∞

*In all your ways **acknowledge** him,*
and he will make your paths straight.
PROVERBS 3:6

*W*here are you now?" the transit authority officer asked. Isn't that always the first question you should ask someone seeking direction? Though many of us would like to get to the corner of Forgiveness and Healing, we find it hard to admit that we are presently standing on the corner of Anger and Pain. Pride becomes a conspiratorial bedfellow, whispering, "Don't ever let them see you sweat."

Yet smothered discomfort finds other ways of manifesting itself. After a demure, "I'm all right," to those closest to us, we snap at strangers, grow impatient with the helpless, cry over trivial trifles, causing others to wonder, "What is up with her?"

There is no way to ignore pain, disappointment, or heartbreak, though Shame tries to tell you otherwise. Shame says you are foolish to feel what you feel. But there is nothing honorable about a cold, dead heart. The ability to love and to give love is a most gracious gift— a gift that some might not be in the position to receive. For this you cannot be blamed or earn the title of fool. Nothing could be further from the truth: this is a lie that insults the heart of God, who is always "guilty" of giving his love, even when we don't love him back.

Where are you? That is the question you need to answer carefully. Lies delay healing. Honesty provides solutions. Aerobics instructors encourage you to "feel the burn." That tells you your muscles are alive and working toward your goal. Yes, pain tells us things. Acknowledge it and listen.

Heartache tells us what is important to us and what we haven't surrendered yet. It tells us what we secretly pine for and openly desire. It exposes our expectations, even the ones we deny, whether they are right or misplaced.

Pain yanks us back to reality. It pulls us off of imaginary clouds. It screams louder than all the whispers that we didn't hear. Pain will not be ignored. It insists we take a closer look. It points an adamant finger at the things that we must fix. It never lets up until we surrender. It is not as patient as God, who waits for us to tell him where it hurts. Pain demands change, or it will scream out again and again, hitting the same spot until we admit where we are and shift position. Pain is … painful. Pain is good. Pain is a teacher. Pain is relentless. Pain directs us back to the right place. Pain leads us to God.

Dear Heavenly Father, I am in pain. I admit it. I hurt. I feel mortally wounded, as if I may never recover. Yet your Word promises healing.

Yesterday I hurt. Today I hurt even more. It seems as if my pain is increasing instead of subsiding. When will the pain end? Help me to endure. There is no place that I can go to separate my heart from myself. I carry it inside of me and it weighs heavily upon me. I don't know if I can carry it any further in its present condition. Where do I turn to escape the pain that is so deep, it is almost physical?

Please, Lord, rescue me from my despair. Touch me and heal me. Dry my tears and restore me. I stand before you naked, hiding nothing, acknowledging my need for healing and redemption. Draw me to yourself and comfort me. Restore my heart and my joy, in Jesus' name. Amen.

15

Call

Call to me and I will answer you and tell you great
and unsearchable things you do not know.
JEREMIAH 33:3

"Why didn't you call me?" my friend said, looking deeply concerned over my distress. To be honest, I had an attitude. I wanted her to have ESP. I wanted her to sense my pain from a distance and reach out to me even though I had not called. I had already been burned for reaching out to someone; I couldn't bear another person refusing my need, even if it was merely a delay.

"Can I call you back?" No, I couldn't even bear that. I wanted immediate attention.

Not only did I want attention, I wanted an answer. An answer that would fix this mess my heart was in. Now that I'd found her and relayed all that I felt, she looked at me, sympathetic but at a loss for words. Not knowing what to say to ease my pain. Shifting through and exhausting every comforting phrase she had in her friendship file, she found them all trite at a time like this. Finally, she opted for, "Have you prayed about it?"

No! I had not prayed about it. In situations like this, God never seems to answer soon enough, or give me the answer I want. No, I had not prayed—and now I was being confronted with the fact that I really had no other choice. No one else had an answer. No one else could get to where it hurt inside of me. They could only guesstimate what I was feeling. They did not know both sides of the story. They could not see the end of the story. They did not have enough information.

"Oh God, help me," was all that I could muster. But it was enough. Perhaps it wasn't about an answer right now. It was more about a little comfort. As I released myself into his arms, a warmth surrounded me and I drifted into an easy sleep. Upon awakening, I felt lighter, more open to other options.

And then the answers began to come, one by one. A revelation here, an understanding there. Slowly they came, like the dawning of an especially crisp, cool day. In subtle colors, growing more brilliant and intense, more clearly defined, over the horizon of my spirit, illuminating the dark corners of my mind. Quietly, as if attempting not to be rude, not insisting that they be heard, the answers came. Some of them I did not like, yet I could not be offended as they politely told the truth.

Perhaps this is why we do not call God. His answers are not like the pacifying answer of a friend who is guilty of partiality. His answers—though wise, honest, and life-giving—also come laden with truth that forces us to take responsibility for our hearts and our lives. His answers always require some sort of change. His answers come charged with details we were not seeking, yet we are the better for it if we take heed.

To forfeit this opportunity is to continue to drive in circles, never reaching our destination because we refuse to stop and ask for directions. "Why didn't you call me?" Such a simple answer for such a complex set of circumstances.

Have mercy on me, O Lord, for I call to you all day long. Bring joy to your servant, for to you, O Lord, I lift up my soul. You are kind and forgiving, O Lord, abounding in love to all who call to you. Hear my prayer, O Lord; listen to my cry for mercy. In the day of my trouble I will call to you, for you will answer me…. Teach me your way, O Lord, and I will walk in your truth; give me an undivided heart, that I may fear your name. I will praise you, O Lord my God, with all my heart; I will glorify your name forever. For great is your love toward me.... But you, O Lord, are a compassionate and gracious God, slow to anger, abounding in love and faithfulness. Turn to me and have mercy on me; grant your strength to your servant and save.... Give me a sign of your goodness, that my enemies may see it and be put to shame, for you, O Lord, have helped me and comforted me.

PSALM 86:3-7,11-13,15-17

Dear Heavenly Father, I am calling....

$\mathcal{B}$e Angry

∞

*"In your anger do **not sin"**: Do **not** let the sun go down*
*while you are still **angry.**…*
EPHESIANS 4:26

$\mathcal{A}$dmit it. You are angry. Angry at yourself for being in this position. Angry at the one who hurt you so thoughtlessly, so selfishly, so heartlessly. Angry at God for not protecting you.

There, I've said it. The unmentionable. Being angry at God.

We tiptoe around that set of emotions and hope they will go away. If we ignore them, perhaps these feelings will fade to black and we will never have to deal with our disappointment in him. We will never have to question his motives. Why did he allow this to happen? Didn't he know how much I would suffer? How can he allow this sort of thing to go on unchecked? How am I supposed to believe he loves me when he allows me to be hurt like this?

We feel justified in our anger at our offender. He is wrong. Wrong to inflict suffering on another human soul. Would he deal as graciously with his pain if the tables were turned? How could he lead your heart down the garden path of trust and then so viciously betray your love?

The bigger question is, why? Whether the situation is rejection, betrayal, or sudden abandonment, the pain and the questions are the same. Couldn't he have done things differently? Shown a measure of kindness or consideration? Given some kind of warning? Let you down a little easier—or not at all?

And what about you? What is your role in this three-part

drama? Were you truly naïve, or oblivious? Blame points an angry finger at you and cries, "It's all your fault, how could you have been so stupid?" How quickly we succumb to false condemnation when we feel we have no one else to blame.

"It's all your fault." Those words echo over and over through the caverns of your soul, burning a hole and leaving permanent imprints in your personality. How many times around this mountain before I get it right? Why didn't I pay attention to the signs along the way? Next time I will be more cautious. No! There won't be a next time.

Now vows are uttered in haste. Walls called "never again" are erected, causing you to feel false comfort and imaginary protection. To remain angry is not to feel. Not to feel sadness, pain … anything. It's better this way. To be separated from one's self. To forbid the heart to breathe. To punish the offender with silence and empty stares. To withhold your heart from God as bribery. Perhaps he will do something now if he really loves you. That's fair. He understands. He can even relate. He knows how it feels to be angry. Angry at the callous waywardness of those he loves. Angry at the rejection of those he deserved attention from.

Yes, God will allow you your moment of anger, if that's what it takes to get you through this moment. He only asks that you not remain there. Like Egypt, anger can quickly turn from a place of sanctuary to a place of bondage if you stay too long. The same place that once fed your soul will force you into thankless labor and oppression.

Anger will smother your ability to praise your God. It will remind you of all the unyielded rights you struggle to surrender. It will cut off your joy and drain you of your strength. It will hinder you from moving on. Therefore it will bind you from receiving the promise.

This is when anger makes the subtle transition, from friend to foe. Anger will not assist you in moving from this place. It will plant its feet in front of you and challenge you to get past it. It will paralyze you with its stare and dare you to look away and hope for a better tomorrow. It invites you to drink the cup of bitterness and swallow its unpleasant nature. To all of these things, say no. Indulge your anger for a moment, then discard him like an unfaithful lover. His intentions toward you are not pure and will birth no good thing. But by all means entertain him for an afternoon.

Vent, scream, rage, let it all hang out, and then usher anger to the door. Then turn and return to the Son before evening sets in. For the way to freedom is more difficult to find in the dark.

Dear Heavenly Father, I am angry. I am angry at you. Angry at the one who offended me. Angry at myself for allowing myself to be victimized. Knowingly or unknowingly, it makes no difference.

Perhaps you tried to warn me and I ignored your still, small voice. Perhaps you said nothing, thinking this was a lesson I needed to learn. Whatever the order of events, I think I am angry at you because I expect you to save me from pain in spite of myself and all that I do. That is probably not fair and a bit presumptuous on my part, but I have to get this off my chest because it is burning down to the core of my being.

I don't understand. I simply don't understand why these kinds of things happen. Will you really let this person get away with hurting me? Why didn't you stop him? How can I praise you when I don't feel I can trust you to protect my heart? And though you have given me the responsibility of guarding my heart, I don't always do a good job. I am still struggling to yield my rights to you completely.

Was I in the way? I thought you would be there in those times to save me when I couldn't save myself. I know that I am supposed to learn something when I go through experiences like these, but right now I see no rhyme, no reason, no lesson. I guess I'm just too angry. I'm so angry it hurts and I know that I cannot stay in this place. Yet I find that my hands are so tightly wound around my pain I can't release it for you to heal it.

Help me to let go. Help me to open my hands. Deliver me from the stronghold of anger and bitterness. Help me to forgive and release the one who hurt me, forgive myself, forgive you. Hold me close and love the hurt away. Help me to endure the pain and move through it, knowing that healing is on the other side, in Jesus' name. Amen.

Out of the depths I cry to you, O Lord;
O Lord, hear my voice.
Let your ears be attentive to my cry for mercy.

PSALM 130:1,2

here is a place beyond numbness and anger where tears abide. Let yourself go there. When there is nothing left to be said, surrender. No help is needed from your intellect, for tears have their own conversation. Though it is not translatable to the human ear, it is not foreign to God because it is the language of truth.

Tears hold no deception. They are transparent, their message clear. They do not cover their pain or paint it a different shade. They do not diffuse the depth of their agony, they are spurred on by it. They rise to the occasion in an attempt to wash away the grime of rejection, the soot of betrayal, the darkness of anguish that cannot be uttered. They press against the walls of our spirit, building and building until the pressure grows too great for pride to withstand. Though they are silent, their presence cannot be ignored. They must be allowed to have their say.

One silent trickle, followed by another drop and then another. Slowly they make their way. Cautiously over the rim of your soul, building in momentum, anxious to rinse your heart from all of its despair. With tears comes release. A sob from somewhere down deep inside the you that you had buried, rises like a yawn after a good sound sleep. It stretches into a wail that totally exposes your suffering. And though you have no words in your vocabulary to describe the way you feel, your tears say it all. They ask no questions. They do not seek understanding. They only express the hidden things of the heart. The things you sought to suppress, for even if you whispered them you would deem them shameful, embarrassing, exposing your own cooperation in your emotional demise, your failure.

But your tears will have no part in rationale. They are pure. They hold no secret agendas. They are real. Tears catch God's attention and hold it. The message they carry is recorded on his scroll and not ignored. They seek no justice, only healing. They expose the brokenness we would rather ignore. They cleanse our hearts and wash our wounds.

So let go. Let the tide rise and do its work. It is no longer about anyone else but you in this moment. Release yourself to the flow and let it carry you to the place of refreshing. And after the river has subsided, you will find that you are left empty, and open to finally hear from God.

Dear Heavenly Father, in my silence hear my unreleased tears. I am spent. Afraid to utter what might lie in the deepest parts of my heart. My pain is so excruciating I feel I must grit my teeth to survive each fresh wave that washes over me. Hold me in the midst of the storm. Grant me the release I need to let my tears flow. As you collect my tears in your bottle, rinse me with them and minister your healing to my wounded heart.

Be my comfort when I weep. Hear the words I am unable to say. Listen to my heart and answer its cry, Lord, for I am devoid of questions or explanations. I just long to be free of my suffering. I don't know what else to say. Respond to my silent petition. Know and understand the language of my upraised arms. My bowed frame. My weeping eyes. Translate my groanings, my sighs, my sobs. And when there's nothing left within me, commiserate with my silence and hold me in your arms. Lord, I have come to the end of myself. Lead me to the beginning of hope renewed, in Jesus' name. Amen.

18

Pray

"Why are you sleeping?" he asked them.
"Get up and pray so that you will not fall into temptation."
LUKE 22:46

*N*o, it's not just you. It is a scientific fact that both trauma to the emotions and overexertion cause physiological depression. Depression protects its children by lulling them to sleep. Like Scarlett O'Hara, we prefer to think about it tomorrow. After all, tomorrow is another day.

However, we don't awaken to find our troubles *Gone With the Wind*. They are still there. And the disappointment of having to face our grief continually can make us willing to do almost anything to relieve the pain. Anything, that is, but pray. "I've said it all, what is left to say?" one reasons. It's as if an invisible vise has clamped your jaws together, making it impossible to eke out even one word to God.

We've all been there. We struggle to render a silent prayer and find ourselves devoid of thought. Not one single intelligent sentence or question comes to mind. One by one, each wordless day goes by with only a vague awareness that another day has passed without talking to God. Another day of suffering in silence.

Like the disciples, we find ourselves in our own personal Gethsemane, bowed over with heaviness, unable to pray, feeling minutes away from death. But to cease to pray now is to disconnect ourselves from the only lifeline we have. If we stop talking with God, we cease to receive his instructions. And once we stop listening for his voice, trust me, there are other voices only too happy to lead us the wrong way.

There is only One who can sedate and heal, bind up and repair even our scars. The enemy wants to keep us separated from the One who has the glue to mend our broken hearts, the only one who can truly put us back together inside, where no one else can see. The circumstance in which you now find yourself may be more about destroying your relationship with God than your dreams.

There is only way to find the right answer to all your questions, and that is to talk to the One who knows. God is a perfect gentleman; he will not answer until we ask. He will not give his opinion without invitation. He will not touch us until we draw near. Prayer is a most necessary ingredient in the salve of healing. All attempts are impotent without it.

So, in spite of your weariness, in spite of your depression, in spite of your feelings of resignation and hopelessness—in spite of it all, pray. In the spirit. In your understanding. Whatever it takes. Just pray.

Dear Heavenly Father, I don't really know what to say. I feel as if I have exhausted my entire vocabulary on this subject. I feel as though I have repeated myself over and over again. Whether with friends or just inside of my own mind. I have wearied myself to the extreme and now I feel depleted. I don't really know what to say to you.

I really need to see you move on my behalf. I need to know that you have seen all that has taken place, and that you will do something about it.

Lord, you know the facts. I have nursed and rehearsed them a thousand times. I find it impossible to figure out why anyone would want to assault my heart and disregard my feelings like this. I ask that you arise, not only as my comforter and healer but also as my defender. Then bring me to the point of closure and release and grant me a new beginning. But most of all, help me to get back to the place of spending consistent time with you. Renew our friendship. Bring a refreshing to my prayer time and release my lips to praise you once again, in Jesus' name. Amen.

$\mathcal{P}$raise

Praise *the Lord, O my soul, and forget not all his benefits.*
PSALM 103:2

$\mathcal{H}$mph! Praise! Funny how that word always pops up when it's the last thing we feel like doing. The enemy of our souls comes sneering, "Praise God for what? For this mess? What's so good about it?"

Indeed, what is good about it? Whatever the circumstance, it is another opportunity for God to show himself strong on your behalf. How can you be sure? Because if you truly reach back into your memory bank, you're sure to withdraw a recollection of God's overwhelming goodness in the midst of a previous trial. Another space in time when you felt that you would surely die. Would never recover. Would never make it through. Make it out. Make it, period!

And yet, you did. By the grace of God, you did. Somehow it worked out. Not only worked out, but worked out for the good. *Surprise, surprise.* When all else fails, God never does.

This is why we must speak truth to ourselves. Not in public, lest we be diagnosed as mad. But in the sanctuary of our own private spaces, in the quiet of our own souls. Rehearse the former graces of God. Recite old testimonies of what he has done before, and if you find nothing then admit that you are ungrateful and begin again.

Yeah, girl, talk to yourself. Talk to your inner man, not that man that did you wrong, but the *inner* man of your spirit. Tell it to line up and fly right. Remind it how to get God's attention. You know, we all feel like extending a little more favor when someone praises us. Praise confuses the enemy and lifts the fog from your soul. It turns the lights back on. It re-ignites hope and gets the angels busy. It stirs up activity in the heavens and makes God lean forward in his throne. Praise raises the roof off of your sorry situation and lets in some fresh air. Take a whiff and feel strength flood through your body.

This is what one must *will* to do. It has absolutely nothing to do with feelings. Feelings are as fickle as fashion, they change from season to season. Feelings are merely deceivers. The coat that covers the real truth. The truth is, no matter what is going on, you will live. You will make it. You will begin again. And no matter how fresh your pain is right now, some day it will be a very faint memory. I guarantee it.

How long you choose to wallow is up to you, but for my money, I think I'll rise up and yank my life back out of the enemy's hands, thank you very much. It is time to change the color in the room, to rearrange one's do. It is time to take over and get back on track. And though you might have to repeat this exercise a couple of times until you make it over, that's all right. Just keep steppin'. Keep praisin'. Keep praisin' in spite of what you see. In spite of what you hear. In spite of what you feel. Just keep praisin'.

Dear Heavenly Father, forgive me for my distance. Forgive me for my ungrateful heart. Somehow I became distracted by my circumstances and forgot about your goodness. So I will to turn my heart toward you now and focus on all that you are to me. Lord, I thank you because you are faithful. You are wonderful. You are patient. You are loving. You are altogether lovely.

I might not be able to see how you can turn this situation to the good right now, but I thank you for all of your promises, which are yea and amen. I thank you that I can cast all of my cares on you because you care for me. I thank you because you are a healer, my comforter, my friend, my provider. Lord, you are the lover of my soul. Great is your faithfulness! Even when I am faithless, Lord, you never give me leftovers. You serve up new mercies every morning. Thank you.

Thank you, Lord, for all that you have done for me. For the blessings seen and unseen I thank you. I lift my hands in praise to you right now and forever. I love you, Lord. I praise you and I give you all the glory, in Jesus' name. Amen.

Love is not synonymous with pain ...
but therein lies the paradox.
The intricate pattern of emotions
that lies within one big word ...
vulnerability ...
not so big after all
but then again not so small
for there lies the secret
ah yes
the thing that brings you the most joy
bears the potential of bringing you the most pain ...
haven't we heard time and time again
love hurts? ...
(a gross miscalculation)
but nevertheless a fair explanation of man's quest for pain ...
in which he finds everything
but that which he seeks.
For love is joy ...
love is life ...
love is God ...
love is selfless ...
and in selflessness there is no pain ...
only death to everything within
except the power to give....
Which could explain our pain ...
our anger
our response
to what we feel are violated rights ...
(Why wasn't my love returned?) ...

(continued on next page)

our self pity ...
our search for an excuse ...
for the reason why ...
(Maybe it was me ...)
our depression ...
the aftermath
the exhaustion of the inward fight ...
(I'm too tired to care anymore) ...
our hopelessness
the rebellion ...
the refusal to regain strength....
(Why should this time be different?) ...
but we live ...
and in spite of ourselves, we learn ...
we stumble
we fall
we are propelled onward
until we grow into the knowledge
that the only painful thing about love
is our misplaced expectations ...
For love is soft ...
and warm ...
love is tough
and strong ...
love is tender and enduring
love is ...
love is ...
love just is ...
but love is not
synonymous with pain....

– 20 –
Repent

Those whom I love I rebuke and discipline.
*So be earnest, and **repent**.*
REVELATION 3:19

They say there are three sides to every story. Your side. The offender's side. And God's side. From where he sits, the view can look quite different. While we point an accusing finger at the person who hurt us, four more fingers point back in our direction.

Generally speaking, yet more often than not, we have played a part in the drama of our hearts. Even if it is something as subtle as staying in a relationship too long, we must take responsibility for not taking better care of ourselves.

So repent.

Even if in good conscience you can clearly state you did nothing to contribute to the painful events that have unfolded, chances are that in the process of separation your heart has turned left instead of right. A vengeful thought. A moment of looking back at something you knew was no good for you. Repent, and get back on the right track.

Repent for giving your heart away too soon. For refusing to pay attention to the signs. For rejecting sound counsel in the name of "you just don't understand." For not inquiring of the Lord. For compromising your walk with God. Your sexuality. Your values. Your faith. For looking for love in the wrong place. For seeking fulfillment from the wrong source. For being so desperate to be loved, to feel "normal," that you let down your guard to embrace a feel-good moment. For snatching your heart out of God's hands to give to one who was undeserving. For failing to wait on God. For failing to trust him to give you a good and perfect gift. For being out of order, spiritually or as a woman.

If any of these sound familiar, repent.

Repent for saying unneeded words at the wrong time—no "ifs," "ands," or "buts." Repent for not listening. For not responding. For being selfish. Oblivious. Insensitive. For waiting too late to do the right thing. For harboring anger and resentment. For beating yourself up. For shaking your puny fist at God. For questioning God's wisdom and resenting his protection. For taking out your pain on innocent bystanders. For nurturing a bad attitude. For refusing to learn the lesson. For refusing to make truth your friend. For speaking evil of the one who hurt you.

Have I hit you yet? Need I go on?

Whatever your part, repent. Whether it is an offense of thought, word, or deed. Repent. Clear your decks. Repent. Not for the sake of your offender. But for the sake of yourself. For your own personal deliverance. Repent that you might live. Make your path straight toward the throne, that the ear of God might be open to you. Accept the chastening of his Spirit. Take responsibility for your actions. And though you might be able to justify whatever you have done to everyone else, you know—*God* knows—the truth.

Place your excuses at the foot of the cross and relinquish them again. No more "let me explain," no more "I thought" or "I didn't think." A good, healthy, "I was wrong" would carry you further right now. Admitting wrong rolls the stone away and gives us access to the only one who can bring life back into a dead situation. God calls us to come. He invites us to reason with him and to allow him to wash us and refresh us. He's always ready to embrace us. Repent. Get over yourself. Let bygones be bygones. Begin again.

Dear Heavenly Father, I must admit I had not stopped to think what I had done wrong in this scenario. I was too caught up in my own pain to notice. All I know is that I was hurting and it was not my fault. Someone had hurt me and I wanted you to get that person. But now I must take a sober look at how I could have contributed to my own pain. Forgive me for taking my own life in my hands and running with it.

Forgive me for expecting more from any man than I do from you. Forgive me for considering the love of another more desirable than yours. For considering his comfort more immediate or more satisfying. Somewhere along the way I stopped heeding your voice and instruction. I refused the counsel of others you sent my way. I danced too near the flame and was burned.

So I ask your forgiveness for anything that I might have done to offend you in thought, word, or deed. I ask that you forgive me for the things I know I shouldn't have done. I ask that you bring to mind anything I have overlooked. Deliver me from impatience and rebellion. From doubt and unbelief. These are the things that urge me toward actions that I know are not conducive to victory in my life. So as I lay these burdens down before you, I ask that you embrace me, wash me, and help me to begin again, in Jesus' name. Amen.

21

Forgive

Do not judge, and you will not be judged. Do not condemn, and you will not be condemned. **Forgive***, and you will be forgiven.*

LUKE 6:37

ow do you begin to forgive someone who has hurt you? Do you begin sifting through your pain to find the one grain of rationale that could excuse the other person's behavior?

The truth is that forgiveness has nothing to do with who is right or wrong. Forgiveness is a free agent. It is not attached to reason or agreement or even understanding. It *is*, however, attached to wholeness, and to your healing and liberation.

Unforgiveness is a prison. It slams the door on new beginnings and entrenches you in your present pain. It chains the heart and stops it from beating. It suffocates joy and paralyzes your ability to move on. Forgiveness is the arthritis of the soul. It slowly eats away the marrow of your existence and impairs your judgment, your personality, and your ability to love again.

The desire to know that the person who hurt us is also hurting can be overwhelming. We become jealous of their joy, wanting them to feel the torture we think they deserve. *How can he act as though nothing ever happened?* we ask ourselves. *It's not fair! Where is God in all this? Is there no justice?!*

Yes, there is justice. But justice comes only after we have released our offender into the hands of the One who is solely in the position to judge. Only God knows both sides of the story. Only he knows the deficiencies of both parties. The fears, the past wounds, the generational conditioning, the weaknesses, the insufficiencies of character and integrity. He knows the things that we in the glow of love failed to notice. The things that should have warned us to guard our hearts.

Only God knows the hidden motives and the unspoken regrets of the one who hurt you. The assumptions we make usually do more damage than the truth:

"He never really cared about me."

"He doesn't even notice how much he hurt me!"

"How could he be so cold?!"

Yes, our imaginations can be unmerciful. Trust me, it's never what you think. Your guesses will always be more cruel than the reality of what really transpired, adding unnecessary injury to insult.

You need to let it go. You need to forgive. Not for his sake—for yours. It's time to redirect your focus and move on. And you won't be able to do that if you continue to nurse and rehearse your anger, the many wrongs done against you, all the reasons why.

If you can't forgive for your own sake, forgive for *God's* sake. He needs your hands open in order to bless you. Cooperate. No one who wronged you *that* much deserves so much of your time or attention. Your fixation is standing in the gap between that person and God, shielding him from conviction. Move out of the way. Free him to receive the proper correction from God.

Forgive because you need to be forgiven. How can you expect what you are unable to give yourself? Forgive, my sister, because you are not alone. We have all been there. So come and join us on the other side.

Dear Heavenly Father, the words don't come easily, but I choose to forgive. I will to forgive because it is what you require of me and it is what is best. Help me to forgive from my heart and not just from my head. Help me to release my offender, for to release him is to release myself. Free me from my anger and my pain. Free me from all the questions that continually assault my mind.

Free me from all of the assumptions that flood my soul. Unwrap my fingers from around my offense. Break the chains off my emotions. Open the prison doors of my indignation and shame. Lead me to a better place. A place where you address all my needs and assure me that you have taken heed to the things that have transpired. Speak words of comfort to me. And though I may never forget what has happened to me, help me to forgive even as you have forgiven me, in Jesus' name. Amen.

22

*B*less

> *But I tell you: Love your **enemies** and*
> *pray for those who persecute you.*
> MATTHEW 5:44

*B*less him! *Now wait a minute, Michelle, you are taking this whole thing too far. First you ask me to forgive this … this … person who has wronged me so terribly, and now you tell me I have to bless him on top of it all?! I'm the one in need of a blessing! Haven't I been through enough?*

I can definitely understand that train of thought, but bear with me. If we are taking the journey toward healing, we cannot skip this step. If we do, we will rob ourselves of the true freedom and wholeness God wants us to embrace. This can be your turning point. Your detour to joy: at every corner, plant what you yourself would like to reap.

Does someone who hurt you deserve to be blessed? We may not think so, but who has the right to say? Perhaps it was the lack of blessing that perverted that other person's character in the first place. A void might have been left empty. A hope denied. A fear allowed to grow. We will never know the true tale, but of one thing we can be sure, somewhere in that person's life is a lack that must be filled. Only the blessed can truly be a blessing to others.

We have been called to bless and not curse. For if you refuse to bless, blessings will elude you. Utter a curse, and you will find it crouching outside your own door. Remember that the power of life and death is in your tongue. Every time you kill another with the words of your mouth, a piece of you accompanies that person to his grave. Don't go there.

Choose pity over anger. It will make you more gracious. Invite mercy to visit you by setting a place for it at your table. Serve mercy, and it will serve you. And when you feel you've exhausted your supply, allow grace to make up the difference. As we will to bless those who have hurt us, the floodgates of forgiveness and healing are unleashed. Peace takes up residence in our inner being.

As we tap into the needs of our offender, we see what we have been spared from and realize that truly we are most blessed! This is when the language of blessing is changed to the language of high praise. Bless God, from whom all blessings flow! No good thing will he withhold from those that walk uprightly before him.

Bless God for every good and perfect gift! He will not settle for less for us, though we ourselves are quick to grasp at common fare. Oh yes, bless God for all he keeps from us, and all he bestows upon us. His intervention and prevention is our greatest protection. Bless God, who is determined to keep your heart from those who are unqualified to hold it.

Bless God, and then bless God some more. When you finally see the big picture, you're going to bless him in hindsight. So, why wait? No matter how you feel right now, bless him as you anticipate a future celebration. So bless God! And bless your offender! Bless him real good. Ask God to give him all the good things that you yourself desire. And then snatch a blessing for yourself. In God's economy, even the bad turns out for the good. And *that* is a blessing.

Dear Heavenly Father, this is difficult, but here goes. I bless _____.
I choose to openly bless and not curse him. Bless this person, Lord,
with a greater knowledge of you and your ways. Increase his under-
standing on the issue of love. Remove the heart of stone within him
and give him a heart of flesh that beats with your love.

Forgive and cleanse all his sin. Let your conviction fall upon
_____, that he might repent and have a new beginning. Make
him a child of grace. Fill the empty spaces within and heal his pain.
Restore his joy and peace, and make him secure in you.

Yes, Lord, regardless of how I feel, I will bless _____ and ask
for your best for him. I was unworthy yet you chose to bless me with
the life of your Son. You chose to sacrifice for me when I took
no notice of you. You chose to give when I took your blessings for
granted. You chose to love me when I wouldn't love you back, but
in the end your goodness captured my heart and made me new. I
pray the same for him, Lord. Meet him in his place of need. Bind
up the broken places in his spirit, sustain and bless him. Help
_____ to be whole and free to give love as you have ordained it, in
Jesus' name. Amen.

Release

*It is for freedom that Christ has **set** us **free**.*
Stand firm, then, and do not let yourselves
be burdened again by a yoke of slavery.

GALATIANS 5:1

*O*nce upon a time there was a young woman who loved to go on long solitary walks in the cool of the evening. One night she was so absorbed in thought, she failed to notice the lateness of the hour or the path she was taking. She slipped and fell, tumbling over the side of a steep hill and grasping the branch of a tree to break her fall.

As she dangled in the darkness she cried, "O Lord, please save me!" In spite of the pain of trying to secure her position and the panic of her circumstance, a voice broke through her inner scrambling. "Let go, my child," it said.

But how could she let go? She would surely die if she had nothing to hold on to. Surely gripping something was better than nothing. And though her arms ached from the strain of struggling to keep herself safe, she was certain that a greater pain awaited her if she released the branch she held.

How far would she fall, if she did let go? She did not know. She could see no further than where she was. And so she determined to hold on as long as she could. Exhausted, yet hoping against hope, she clung to the only sure thing she knew.

The hours went by excruciatingly until at last the sun began its ascent to usher in the day. The woman, now wracked with pain from holding on so long, was astounded to find that her suffering had been completely unnecessary. For not six inches away from her feet was solid ground.

So many times we hold on much longer than we should. Painfully. Unnecessarily. Nursing and rehearsing what the other party did to assault our hearts. We cling to a relationship gone wrong or to romanticized memories of that which is no longer, afraid that if we release them we will have nothing left to talk about. It is difficult to see on the other side of the darkness. Around that distant corner.

What does the future hold? Will there be someone to love and protect me the way I've always longed to be loved and protected? Or will my life become a vast wasteland of nothingness?

"Perhaps I should cling to the little I do have, and be satisfied," we sigh. However, by refusing to release those memories, and unfruitful relationships, or simply dressing up our memories of love gone awry and living off them for a season, could prevent us from discovering the gift God has for us. But holding on only leaves us with empty, aching arms. Hearts too fatigued to hope anymore. Spirits grown dry from the despondency that comes from not moving forward.

Let go. Whatever you're clinging to, let it go. The anger. The longing. The dismay. The questions. Don't try to figure it out. What went wrong. Who was right. Don't try to make sense of it. There is probably no explanation that could satisfy you right now.

Let go. Do not allow yourself to be dragged through regrets and other unvictorious patterns. To hold on is to be held captive by your offender's lack of regard, or enslaved by your own disappointment and ravaged self-esteem. To hold on is to bind yourself to all that will hinder you from receiving the things you long for.

Remember—today will soon pass. Prior experience has shown

that it is possible to love again. After we bleed and we heal, we will live to use once-damaged members again. Do not fear the unknown. Embrace it, for it offers escape from your pain. But before you can take hold of tomorrow, you must let go of today.

It's your choice. When you grow sick and tired of being sick and tired, push the plate away and select from another menu. Choose your thoughts and conversations wisely. Close your eyes, open your hands, and dare to taste something new. Believe that Papa has something better to serve than what you've already tasted. Let him take that old plate away and give you something fresh. Something you can feel. Something that will stick to your ribs. Something that will finally satisfy your deepest longings. Something real.

Let go, girl. Hanging on won't change a thing. It will only deepen your embarrassment. You are not the first one to make a mistake, and you won't be the last. You're more normal than you think, 'cause it's been proven, the counterfeit always comes before the blessing. So face the music, whether you like the song or not. Call the entire experience exactly what it was. A passing moment of deception designed to trip you up. Don't let it. Let it go.

Dear Heavenly Father, this is really hard. Letting go feels as if I am admitting defeat, as if I am surrendering my faith in you to work this matter out. It is a scary thought, letting go. I don't know what is in store for me. I am afraid of being empty. Of being in want. Of being alone. I need the assurance that you will catch my open hands and fill them.

Come and rescue me, Lord. Give me the courage I need to let go. Give me your arm, your hand, anything that I can grip to steady myself. Let me know that in you I have something to hold on to. You will never leave me hanging. Never leave me wondering. Never leave me alone.

Lord, help my unbelief. I admit that the greatest reason I won't let go is because I don't trust you to replace what you take away. In spite of my mistakes, I am afraid to let you choose for me. I don't know why I don't believe that your choices for me will bring me delight. I don't know why I struggle with releasing my life to you, but I do. So now I confess my fear and choose to let go. I have clung to the wrong things long enough. So now I release the one who hurt me. My past, my future, my today. All that I fight to control. I release my desires and dreams. I release myself back into your safekeeping. I choose to cling to you and only you, both now and forever, in Jesus' name. Amen.

For everything I've ever tried to hold,
I have a scar.
A scar from the struggle it took
to secure
what didn't want to stay
For everything I've ever sought to possess
I have wounds
deep, empty ones
betraying what I would rather keep secret
private disappointments
public rejections
and barren hopes ...
spurned affections
adulterous hearts
that stumbled in their faithfulness
to my affections.
I have cried,
I have wept over spilled love
cut myself on the shards of a broken heart
and watched my emotions bleed
into every situation thereafter.
In struggling to stop the flow,
I bandaged myself in layers of denial
only to find
the scars still there
when I deemed it safe to look ...
new prospects picked at the scabs

reopening old wounds
and leaving deeper evidence
of my previous pain.
oh no there is no denying
I've tried to possess some hearts in my time
and found them all slippery
too slippery to hold
and call my own ...
and at the end of the day
the only thing that remains
in my complete possession
is my heart
and the ability to make better choices ....

24

ℬe Silent

☙

In your anger do not sin; when you are on your beds,
*search your hearts and be **silent**.*

PSALM 4:4

Ssh. Don't say a word. Not one syllable. Nothing else needs be said. There is a time to speak and a time to be silent. The time is now. Let it go. Let it rest. Take the spoon out of the pot and stop stirring. Be silent and wait.

Ssssh. You've said enough. It's all been said. Opinions. Conclusions. Turned this way and that. Examined under the microscope of all your friends. Magnified in your mind. Prodded by your spirit from every angle.... That's enough. Don't give it more glory than it's worth. If it is not pure, lovely, or praiseworthy, then say nothing. Don't give the situation any more leeway to master you and control your thoughts. Clip the wings of the devil. Give him no more power to fly. Uh-uh, not even a "but..."

Sssh. Let it go. Refuse to discuss it any longer, no matter how much you are tempted—by others, by yourself, or by the enemy of your soul. Words give life and power to everything they touch. They give wing to things continuing that are better left to die peacefully.

Sssh. God wants to say something. But he won't interrupt you. He won't shout. Won't scream. Won't insist on being heard. Won't force you to see things his way. He will wait politely for you to come to the end of yourself.

Ssssh. It's all right to run out of words. Be empty of explanations. At the end of all our wisdom lies the answer. In the place where God whispers words of comfort. Secrets he has never before revealed. But you must be silent to hear.

So now that you've had your say, it's God's turn. Now that you've exhausted all avenues of exploration, sought advice from the best facilitators, it's time to hear from the only One who has the answer. So stop. Be silent. Take a seat and wait before the Lord. Wait and do not move. Do not speak if he takes too long to answer you. Let the storm subside and the dust settle around you. Let all outside noise diminish and dwindle to nothing. Let all others cease from opinions and prophecies. Call a halt to it all. Tune into his still, small voice and listen. Uh, uh, uh … Sssh.

Stay until you hear his voice. Empty yourself of every ready answer and reaction. Quiet your heart. Still your mind. Hold your tongue. Bask in the silence. For only when we cease from laboring with words, will we be able to hear and know.

Dear Heavenly Father. I am listening.… Speak to me now. Cause me to hear and know what you want me to understand. I now turn my full attention toward you and await your word, in Jesus' name. Amen.

$\mathscr{L}$isten

But whoever listens to me will live in safety
and be at ease, without fear of harm.
PROVERBS 1:33

$\mathscr{L}$isten to the silence. It is pregnant with wisdom. Listen to the voice of the Holy Spirit within. First whispering, then growing louder as you turn your heart to hear. Starting from the beginning, leaving no stone unturned he comes, bearing complete answers. Filling in the gaps left by unanswered questions. Telling you things that you do and *do not* want to hear. Words of comfort and correction. After all, the truth is a double-edged sword. It doesn't play favorites.

Listen. Listen for God. With no preconceived notions, just listen. Unconditionally. With no guidelines. For when you seek to hear his voice above all other things, he comes bearing all that you were seeking. Allow God to reveal the secret motives of the heart. Let him disclose the purpose of the suffering. If you truly listen, you will be able to celebrate your pain. Celebrate it, plant it, and nurture it in ground now fertile from suffering and watered by your tears.

Yes, plant it, let it rest and reap the fruit. Reap it and share it with others, that they might be healed. Rehearse what you have heard and spread it abroad. Let your trial be a tool of healing for others, and in the healing be healed.

Dear Heavenly Father, forgive me for not taking the time to listen to you. In my haste to snuff out the pain of my situation, I forgot to turn to you. Sometimes when I cannot see you or hear your voice, I grow impatient and begin to search for immediate solutions. But these are only Band-Aids, temporary help. In the end, all roads lead back to you.

Lord, you alone can give me understanding and closure. Speak to my heart. Speak to my shattered spirit. Speak words of life and insight, revelation, and wisdom. Grant me understanding. Give me direction. Show me where to go from here. I know that the truth can be painful, but I choose to embrace all that you say, realizing that only the truth can make me free. Prepare my heart to receive your word in its totality, painful lumps and all. I stand open to your correction and guidance. Speak Lord, for your servant is listening, in Jesus' name. Amen.

$\mathcal{L}$earn

Whoever gives **heed** to **instruction** prospers,
and blessed is he who trusts in the Lord.
PROVERBS 16:20

$\mathcal{P}$ay attention to the voice of the Lord. To hear and not learn is to despise your own soul, to damage your own heart. Every time that God speaks, it requires change on our part. He calls for us to turn and take a new path. Difficulty and trial, opposition and hindrance are only detours, signaling the soul to move in a different direction. To come up a little higher, draw a little closer to the center of the Compass of our lives.

It's time to follow. Not blindly, or by rote. With all the "getting" of life, it's when we gain understanding that things begin to change in our world. We must turn toward the Son and chart a new road if we are to fulfill our destiny, which is righteousness, peace, and joy in the Holy Ghost. This is the place of ultimate fulfillment and dreams come true.

Insisting on our own way will never lead us there. Continuing down the same old path, expecting different results each time, is unrealistic as well. So learn at the feet of the Master. Embrace his words. Digest them and let them become a part of you. Allow yourself to be transformed by the renewing of your mind. The past and the future can never be friends because they go in different directions. So acknowledge today and the newness it brings. Release it in the evening and anticipate a different tomorrow.

Learn to admit your mistakes. Only then can anything be

fixed. Learn which doors lead to destruction and avoid them at all costs. Remember, the choice is yours. Learn how to guard your heart and all that is precious to you. Then you will avoid the abuse and disrespect of the undiscerning. Learn of God. For those who know their God will be strong and do exploits. They will avoid cloaked and apparent dangers and save their own souls.

Learn God's Word through and through. It will be a light for you to walk by. Learn God's intentions toward you. Forsake men who do not agree. Learn what you deserve in light of his love for you. Do not settle for less. Learn, and then learn some more, my sister, because in the end the knowledge that God gives will be the source of power that rearranges your tomorrows.

Dear Heavenly Father, I empty myself before you, casting down old habits, both familial and individual. I know I can no longer do things my way. I cannot solve my problems in my own strength. Neither can I be the source of my own healing.

Today I choose to do things your way. Teach me, and I will hear and learn and follow. Lord, lead me to the place that is higher than where I presently reside. Though this place is familiar, help me to trust you as you lead me to a better space. I must admit that though this place is painful, it is all I know. Take my hand and gently walk with me.

I am relying on your patience as never before. Show me the way I must take to find joy; I know you know the route well. Direct me toward your peace and surround me in it. Help me to hide your word in my heart. As I determine to live by it daily, honor my efforts with restoration and healing. Visit me, talk to me, and help me to begin anew, in Jesus' name. Amen.

$\mathcal{M}$ake a Sacrifice

∞

The Lord is God, and he has given us light;
*Bind the festival **sacrifice** with cords to the horns of the altar.*
PSALM 118:27, NASB

$\mathcal{N}$ow you've finally reached the end of yourself. The mist has lifted. The clouds have parted. The other side is in clear view. Before you take another step, throw yourself on the altar. Hold on to it tight and make a sacrifice to God. Take all of the hard things that life has thrown in your direction and build an altar with them. Let them be the foundation of all that you offer to the One who can redeem your suffering. Then cleanse your flesh with your tears and present every broken piece to the Lord with thanksgiving. Thank him for his faithfulness. For his tender mercies. For his everlasting love. For his healing virtue. Thank him simply because he is Lord through it all.

Yes, through it all he is still Lord. A Lord who honors the sacrifice made with a broken spirit and a contrite heart. He draws close to the brokenhearted, so close you can feel his breath upon your face. Giving you new life if you breathe it in. There, there now, this too shall pass.

Render a sacrifice. Place your heart, your body, your soul, your mind, and your strength upon the altar that you have built. Give it all back to him. He will take it and make something glorious. And as your praise lights a fire beneath all that you've laid before him, the aroma of your offering fills his nostrils with a pleasing fragrance. The scent of your presence. Mmmm, you are home. Nothing pleases him more.

Spirit and presence join together, closing the space between, and become one. One in spirit. You are no longer alone in your pain, for God dwells in the midst of the praise of his people.

So praise him through the heartache. Praise him for the experience. This is a true sacrifice. Praise him because he will render something good out of it, though at the moment it is not apparent. Praise him because he's there to help you collect the damaged pieces and put them back together again. Praise him because he has never forsaken you, and because he never will. Praise him because you know of One who is faithful. He will never lie. He will never let you down. Praise him because he is the one thing in life of which you can be sure.

Consider his goodness, and praise will no longer be a sacrifice.

Dear Heavenly Father, I lay my all before you now and offer them to you as a sacrifice. And with my offering I present my praise. Take my heart that I have too often taken from your safekeeping and given to others. Take my mind, blot out the memories of painful yesterdays and fill it with thoughts of you. Take my soul and claim it as your own. Take my strength, for in my weakness you are made strong in me. I need you more than I thought, Lord, and I am willing to confess that.

I sacrifice even my pride to you. The longing for love that I've so fervently held for my own. Yes, even my dreams, Lord, I give them all to you. Take all of me, for without you I am nothing. Let your Spirit overshadow and fill me with yourself, then pour me out as an offering unto yourself. You willingly give yourself to me. Oh, who am I that I should be considered worthy of such greatness? And yet I have settled for so much less. Forgive me, Lord, and accept my sacrifice, as tattered as it may be, for it is all that I have. And all I have I give to you now, in Jesus' name. Amen.

28

Change Your Confession

⬿∞⬿

But can I say just anything?
I must speak only what God puts in my mouth.
NUMBERS 22:38

*A*ll is well," she said as she went her way. She had left her dead son lying on his bed as she went in search of the prophet. So goes the story of the bereaved mother in 2 Kings chapter 4. Just when she had accepted the fact that she would never have children, just when she had chosen to make the best of her life as it was, the prophet had come prophesying something of which she had no longer dared to dream.

She would have a son by this time next year. A special blessing for being such a gracious hostess.

She pleaded with him not to wake this dormant desire within her, lest she begin to nurse and rehearse this longing to the point of misery, as in earlier years. Don't make promises that can't be kept. She had finally grown content. Yet the child came, just as she had been told.

About the time that she had finally reconciled that this was not a dream, that the boy she held in her arms was indeed her son, he died. Yet she refused to grieve. No, no, no. This was unacceptable. How could God be so cruel? Would he give gifts and take them back again? No, she would not even confess what her eyes saw. She would speak only words of faith and require that God honor them. He said that she would have a son, and have a son she would.

So she laid him gently on his bed and went to the source. The one who had prophesied this son in the first place. There was no need to waste words along the way. Murmur to those who could do nothing. No. This was between her, God, and the prophet. To all who questioned her along the way, she had one thing to say. "All is well." And indeed, in the end, it was. The prophet accompanied her home and her son was raised from the dead.

If God is in it, "all is well." If he started the relationship, he will conclude the matter. If your relationship has been shattered, *still* "all is well." Why? Because all things work to the good for those who love the Lord and are called according to his purpose, that's why.

Sometimes loss saves us from a greater pain. Allow God to give and take away what he must to bring you to your determined end. In spite of what your eyes see, what your heart feels, what your flesh desires, "all is well." God is still in control. You can bank on it. Nothing gets past his desk without his permission. And though not all things are within his will, he uses it all for your growth and his glory. Oh yes, definitely, "all is well."

You had better change your confession, girl. Your words have the power of life and death. Which would you rather speak into your situation? No matter how torn you feel inside right now, march up to your mirror and speak to yourself. "Be still, my heart, all is well. Stop weeping, eyes, all is well. Come back, strength, all is well. Rest, weary mind, all is well. Bless the Lord, O my soul, all is well!"

Yes, all is well! God is still on the throne, his ear remains attentive to my cry. He will leave no concern unaddressed. Yes, he is working it out. And what he begins is already finished and good.

So you feel that God has offered you a lollipop and then snatched it back? That all your dreams have come crashing down around you? That he has broken his promise of love and joy to you? That you could just as well give up and die? That your heart will never recover from this blow?

Stop and think again. "All is well." No matter what. Repeat not what your eyes see, but what the Spirit is saying. "All is well."

Dear Heavenly Father, I don't understand why things happened the way they did, but I choose to trust you. To look for your hand in the matter. For I know that if you are near, then all is well. No matter what I feel or see right now, I know that you know the plans you have for me. Plans that are for good and not for evil. Plans to give me a future and a determined end.

I know that you love me and that you only want the best for me. Every good and perfect gift. Grant me the heart to trust you completely and not waver in the face of adversity. Keep me focused on the fact that you know all, and out of that knowledge you make decisions on my behalf. Even when I do not comprehend them, I must trust and rest in your care.

Help me to know when I should hold on and when I should let go. Help me not to murmur and confess negative things. Change my confession. Teach me to repeat only what you say. Words of life. Help me, Lord, to wait on you. And when my flesh grows weary, let me remind myself that because you are Lord, all is well, in Jesus' name. Amen.

Christ bled
    Christ died
        Christ rose again ...
the day he crushed my heart
    in the palm of his hand
        I bled
    and when he threw my love back in my face
I died
    but I will rise again.
I will rise
    shake off the dust
        and start again
            and though I might return to this place
        again and again
    until I get it right
I will face the reality that
    I will bleed
        I will die
            I will rise again
                stronger and better than before.
Such is the cycle of life and love
    to be blessed
        and broken
            and given ...
yes
    Christ bled
        Christ died
            Christ rose again
        and now he lives in me ...
    and in being one with him
I too will bleed
    I will die
        and I will rise again....

29

ℛise and Shake Off the Dust
∞

Shake off your dust; rise up, sit enthroned, O Jerusalem. Free yourself
from the chains on your neck, O captive Daughter of Zion.
ISAIAH 52:2

𝒯he story is told of a mule that fell down an abandoned
well. The hole was too deep to retrieve the unfortunate
animal so, in an effort to put it out of its misery quickly, the
farmer called all of his friends together to help him bury the
mule.

As the men gathered together and began pitching dirt into
the hole, the mule panicked and shook it off, then stepped up
on the freshly fallen mound in an effort to free its feet. With
each shovel full this process was repeated, until—lo and
behold!—the mule was out of the hole and standing on solid
ground!

The moral of the story? Shake it off and step up, sister! Don't
allow yourself to be buried in your pain. Shake it off. Relax,
relate, and release. It can't stick to you unless you allow it to stay.
The hole might feel deep, but God will make a way out. Take it
a step at a time. You will need to cooperate with the process, of
course. When he extends his hands to you, grab his arm, step up
into those strong hands and allow him to lift you to a higher
place.

After you have shaken off the dust, don't forget to bathe in his
rivers of refreshing and finish your toilette with his special brand
of perfume. Essence of Joy. Yes, it is true, it is a costly fragrance.

Costly because it comes from specially selected petals that have been crushed to extract the oil. You have been crushed. Don't waste a drop of what you've bled. Make it an expensive tribute to what you've endured, and let others enjoy your scent.

Though your heart has been crushed by a natural lover, you are still betrothed to a King. Rise up and take your place. Hold your head high. Stand erect and know that you are loved and desired. Free yourself! Break the chains of defeat, resignation, self-hatred, and failure from your neck.

This day you can choose for yourself blessings over curses, life over death, joy over sorrow, victory over defeat, freedom over bondage, love over rejection. Use all that you have learned. Promise yourself never to return again to the place where your garments were soiled. Place your heart in your Father's safe-keeping, and allow him to guard your affections from this day forward.

Dear Heavenly Father, though I have felt covered by the soot of my experience, wash me and refresh me. I know that some action is required by me in order to attain freedom from my pain. Strengthen my arms to hold on to you. Strengthen my legs to come up higher. Draw me close to you.

I choose now to cast off the debris that threatened to smother my spirit. I cast down the power of rejection, abuse, hurt, anger, unforgiveness, and bitterness from my life. I declare that they will no longer reign over me. I will to lift up my head above my enemies and live in triumph. I decree that no weapon the enemy has formed against me shall prosper. No longer will I be held captive by the lies of the enemy. I will embrace your truth, Lord, and cleanse myself in it. I will drink long and deep from your Spirit.

Even now I feel rivers of living water welling up inside of me. Spring up, O well, and cleanse my soul. Spring up, O well, and make me whole. Yes, I declare this day that I am free from all that binds me, in Jesus' name. Amen.

30

ℛebuild

*I will **build** you **up** again and you will be rebuilt, O Virgin Israel.*
Again you will take up your tambourines and
go out to dance with the joyful.

JEREMIAH 31:4

*I*n the book of Ezra, the people of Israel had finally laid the foundation of the temple in order to rebuild it. The priests and others who had seen its former glory wept as they recalled it. The joy and anticipation of once again having a place to worship God was mingled with the sad realization that the temple could never again be restored to its former grandeur. Long ago their enemies had looted this holy place and carried off the best of its ornamentation. These things were lost forever, never to be recovered again. So steeped were they in their own thoughts, they failed to see that now the most spectacular appointment of the temple would be the presence of God himself.

We are now living temples of the Lord. Like the temple, when we walked in our own strength, we adorned ourselves with our own confidence and beauty. God has allowed us to be broken in order that we might learn to rely on the beauty that emanates from his presence in us. It is his confidence and strength that others should behold. His light that will attract others to us.

We must all be leveled from time to time in order to return to the basics. It is in him that we live, we move, we have our very being. In him we have the capacity to love. Having confidence in anything else makes us easy targets for the enemy of our souls.

Where do we begin to reclaim the pieces of ourselves? How do we piece them back together? That is not our job. Let the pieces fall where they may. There is a Master builder in the house, ready and prepared to rebuild your broken heart and re-lay the foundation of your shattered spirit.

Let him do his work. You may not look the same when he is finished with you, but your frame will be greater. You will become a building with character rather than a sterile shell with walls that hold no comfort. Allow him to fill every crack with his Spirit and make you every whit whole. Now you are a worthy temple.

Resist the urge to build on a ruined foundation. Bad foundations make unstable buildings that eventually cave in. Yes, allow yourself to be leveled. Let him start from scratch, and fashion you according to his original design: a house of honor filled with his glory for all to see.

Dear Lord, here I stand, gazing at the ruins of my heart and wondering if I am truly ready to face my future. I am not sure where to begin. I release each piece I've gathered and hold them up to you. You are my Creator, I am an earthen vessel in need of repair. I place myself willingly upon your potter's wheel and submit myself to your healing touch. Make me and mold me, fashion me according to your design.

I admit that in the past I have crawled off the wheel, only to find myself unfinished and unprepared to hold that which you wanted to pour into me. Instead I found myself wanting and willing to accommodate things that were not in accordance with your will for my life. I ask that you pour me out and begin again. Give me a new foundation and grant me greater fortitude. Shape me into a vessel made for your honor. Prepare me to be a sanctuary for you. A glorious temple in which you are pleased to abide, where your glory is evident to all.

Lord, I will cease to struggle against your touch and yield to your hand. Prepare me to contain all that you have for me without fear or apprehension. I present myself as a living sacrifice unto you now. Have your way, do what you will with me, in Jesus' name. Amen.

31

Commit Your Way

ॐ

*Into your hands I **commit** my spirit;*
redeem me, O Lord, the God of truth.

PSALM 31:5

*I*f you've been behind the wheel of your life all this time, the
thought of handing over the keys to God may frighten you
at first. But now that the car has been totaled, are you willing to
let him drive?

Move over. Give him the wheel. After all, he is the wheel in the
middle of the wheel. Who would better know the direction you
should be going? Let him steer your life back on course and keep
you there.

Give in to his direction. Follow where his finger points. He
won't lead you wrong. He knows what's up ahead. Every twist,
every turn, every dry place, every mirage. Trust him to make the
crooked places straight, the rough places smooth. Trust him to
lead you to green pastures, beside still waters, to a place where
there is rest for the weary soul, the healing heart, and restoration
for the spirit.

Commit all that you are and desire to him. He is able to keep
it safe. To preserve you unto the day when all you crave will be
delivered. Don't crawl down out of his lap. Lay your head against
his breast and rest. Leave it all to him. Lose yourself in his
embrace and find yourself where you've always wanted to be.
Safe. Loved. Totally fulfilled. Concern yourself with only him,
and he will do the rest. After all, your business is his business. He
is interested in every part, especially the affairs of your heart.

Go ahead, hand it over. You can trust him at the controls of your heart. He won't allow anyone undeserving, unable to recognize your value, behind the wheel. Oh no, only to the one who can afford the priceless treasure that you are, will the key to your affections be given. A king's ransom must be paid. Let him handle the transaction. Strike no cheap bargains. He knows your worth. Take no failed sale personally. He will only release you to the one who is willing to give his all. Even as Jesus gave his all for you.

Dear Heavenly Father, I admit that far too often I have taken my life into my own hands in the past. I have found out too late that I have chosen the wrong direction for myself. That I have settled for less than you intended for me. To be quite honest I have made a mess of things.

I surrender. I am weary and worn and am no longer interested in doing your job; it is too much for me to bear. So I stand before you, emptied of my own ideas and agendas and recommitting my affairs back to you. Direct me in the way that I should take, and help me to move according to your will. Help me to work with you as you unfold your plan for me.

Help me to relax. With trembling fingers I lay down the last of my human efforts before you. I know you can be trusted with all of my tomorrows, and that you will let me know what I need to know, when I need to know it. Help me to take it one day at a time, in Jesus' name. Amen.

$\mathcal{B}$egin Again

No one sews a patch of unshrunk cloth on an old garment.
If he does, the new piece will pull away from the old, making the
tear worse. And no one pours new wine into old wineskins.
If he does, the wine will burst the skins, and both the wine and the
wineskins will be ruined. No, he pours new wine into new wineskins.

MARK 2:21-22

$\mathcal{L}$et's start over. Out with the old. In with the new. Wipe the slate clean and start from scratch. "Today is the beginning of the rest of your life" … remember that saying? Well, it's true. That glorious day you first accepted Christ as your Lord and Savior, the old you died and you were made new. At that time he cast all of your mistakes into the sea of forgetfulness, never to remember them. The good news is that every day he once again extends to you the opportunity to begin again.

Don't try to do a patch job on the past. It is too much work and it ends up being too expensive. Get yourself a new today. By his Spirit you can afford it. Get a new attitude. Get a new do, too, if that's what it takes. Today do something to signify that this is a new you. The world had better look out!

Now, everyone won't be ready for this. There will always be opposition before receiving a blessing. But God has equipped you to deal with any giants that may try to block your way. Whip them and move on. It's called taking your life back. Negative confessions, references to what used to be and what usually happens, have no future where you're going. Don't entertain them or invite them along. They will only hinder your progress. You've been round this mountain long enough. It's time to strike out for new territory!

This is the day that the Lord has made, so rejoice and get on with it! Dare to do something you've never done before. Revel in a new experience. The possibilities are endless. Dare to hope again. To try again. To love again. God has given you the grace to do so.

Remember, trials will come. They are necessary for our growth. So don't be surprised by them. Learn to ride your storms and master them. Use them to propel yourself to the next level. Renew your mind. Renew your spirit. Renew your view of life, girl!

Yesterday was yesterday. It's over. It's gone. Your love was not wasted. Because Love himself abides in you, you have an endless supply. Pour a new glass and give it to someone in Jesus' name. Go ahead, feel free to start over. You've lived, you've loved and learned. Now it's time to "work whatcha know." So chart your course and set sail, 'cause, girlfriend, it's a new day and a different wind is blowing.

Dear Heavenly Father, new beginnings are scary but I believe I'm ready. Right now I choose to start afresh with you. I ask you to accept my repentance, to wash me and be Lord of my life as never before. Because of your blood old things have passed away and all things have become new. Because of you I am a new creature. By faith I take hold of my new day and my new beginning.

I embrace the chance to start again. I will not draw back from opportunities to love because of past pain. I will renew my commitment to love as you love. I now rest assured that my heart is in your safekeeping and I have nothing to fear. And so I turn, leaving my past behind and looking toward my future with all of its wonderful possibilities. I look to the hills from whence comes my help. My help lies in you, Lord, so take my hand and lead me onward and upward, in Jesus' name. Amen.

The Promise

We've all been disappointed at some time in our lives. We've been misled, purposely or unconsciously. We have all stood staring in disbelief at the remains of discarded promises that were made but never kept. The struggle to begin again is a real one when you don't know where to drop your anchor.

The heart has a million questions, each one defying your desire to continue on. Love again? Forget it! Why try again? Why believe again when it's been proven you have no guarantees? Why risk your heart's safety once more? Yet it is in daring to leap out in faith that the things we desire are gained.

Where to put our trust becomes the great question. How do we know that we will heal? Live? Love again? Finally be loved in return, the way you've always wanted to be loved? Should the promises of a man be taken to heart? How can they be when the record of failure has been so devastating?

Perhaps this is where the adjustment should be made. The focus of our faith has everything to do with where we go from here. Will man be our focus, or God? It always comes down to the same sobering bottom line.

The only place our heart is safe is in the hand of God. The only One we can really believe in is the only One who cannot lie. His promises are yea and amen. He doesn't change his mind. He stands in the gap, making up for all the promises that men have broken. He exchanges those discarded vows with his own assurances. And when he speaks, what he says he will surely do. Believe it.

$\mathcal{I}$ Will Hear

Before they call I will answer; while they are still speaking I will hear.
ISAIAH 65:24

$\mathcal{I}$ sat in my office, numb from the conversation I had just finished. I couldn't cry. I couldn't scream. Though I hurt all over, I couldn't locate where the pain was coming from, to press on it. Brenda slipped soundlessly into my office, sensing that something was wrong. She listened as I tearlessly shared my news. When I had finished my whispered pronouncement, she soundlessly put her arms around me and wept.

Her compassion turned the faucet on my heart, releasing my heartbreak to flow out in a rush of deep sobs that must have risen from my toes. Nothing had changed, yet I was strangely comforted. Brenda not only heard what I said, she felt my pain. She experienced the fellowship of my suffering.

Something special and unspeakable happens when a person feels what you're saying. It opens the door to a healing river. The exchange of pain. The vocalizing of things beneath the surface. Allowing the air to touch your wounds. It washes and refreshes bleeding hearts. And binds up the place that feels the void of loss. Perhaps you are not as alone as you thought....

Even when we are unable to connect with another human being, we are never alone in this world. There have been times when I have poured out my soul to the Lord and heard his Spirit direct me to a scripture that echoes my exact emotion. This is his way of saying, "I know how you feel." That's what God does. He not only hears, he feels our grief. He gives ear not only to our words, but to our silence. He attends to our tears and translates the soundless language of our pain.

When no words can be found to express our anguish, he knows what we are feeling, for he understands the inner workings of the heart. In his omniscience he knew of this moment and was prepared to comfort you long before your spirit felt the lash of offense. He was there longing to shield you from the suffering, weeping for you, stretching out his grace to cover your heart. Snuffing out the sting of the enemy's arrows that were aimed, not to simply wound, but to kill you. Yes, he was there. And he is there still.

This is not the time to turn away. Turn back to the One who is listening to even the things that you cannot bring yourself to say.

Dear Lord, I am so grateful that you not only hear me, but that you feel my pain. It is in this place that I feel close to you. It comforts me to know that you collect my tears and pay attention to every sigh. That the Holy Spirit interprets the cries of my heart when I cannot vocalize them myself. And that you come bearing not just compassion but healing.

Gather me in your arms now and love the hurt away. Speak to me through your word and remind me of the promises I need right now to make it through. Help me to release all my pain into your hands, and my heart into your safekeeping. Lord, thank you for feeling what I am unable to say, in Jesus' name. Amen.

– 34 –

I Will Answer

*Call to me and I will **answer** you and tell you*
great and unsearchable things you do not know.

JEREMIAH 33:3

*W*hen you are really ready to know the truth, God will
introduce you to it. Until then, he will wait. He won't
push, won't force you to look into light too bright for unprotected eyes.

Ah, but when we finally decide to emerge from the River of
Denial and wrap ourselves in the towels he extends to warm and
dry us, he gently begins to peel back layers of deception that hid
the answers our hearts should have asked for earlier.

It's "better late than never" where truth is concerned. Truth is
the only thing that makes every wounded soul free. God knows
this. And so he will wait for you until you are ready to receive it.
As long as it takes, he will wait. Wait for your call. Wait for your
"Yes, I am ready, tell me all you know."

It is wise to call upon the Lord. It is wiser still to seek the truth
he offers, for truth and wisdom are friends. They remain faithful
to you in your pain unless they are pushed away. Don't waste a
grain of your pain. Learn from it. Force it to tell you all the things
you didn't know that brought you to this place. The deep inner
secrets of your own heart. Your weaknesses. Your vulnerabilities.
The cracks in your armor. The secrets of your spirit. The needs
you didn't know you had. The strengths you've never recognized
or exercised.

Yes, now is the time to listen intently. God has so much to share. Go ahead. Call him. Ask him all your really hard questions. I guarantee his answers will surprise you.

Dear Heavenly Father, I admit I have not given you my full attention in this matter. Perhaps I thought the truth would be too painful. But what could surpass the pain I feel now? If it is truly the truth that will set me free, then give it to me now. I need to see clearly. I need to hear your heart on this matter.

Show me my own mistakes. What doors I opened for this to come upon me. Forgive me for shutting you out instead of seeking you.

Forgive me for not being willing to hear everything you had to say. I confess that I was afraid to listen. I wanted this to work so badly, I feared even your interruption. So here I am, back at your feet. Heart in hand, soul in tremendous pain, awaiting your word to comfort me and make sense of all that has happened. You alone know, even as you knew all along.

So although I'm late, I am here. Ready and willing to attend to your word. Speak, Lord, and I will hear, in Jesus' name. Amen.

$\mathcal{I}$ Will Draw Near and Reveal Myself
∞

*"I will bring him **near** and he will come close to me, for who is he who will devote himself to be close to me?" declares the Lord.*

JEREMIAH 30:21

$\mathcal{W}$ ho is he or she indeed? More often than not, it is those who have been broken, bruised, or crushed. Those whose souls have been assaulted, whose wounds go deeper than they can physically touch. These are the ones who draw close to the Lord. When all else has failed them, they grasp the one constant who never fails. And he is faithful to respond. Kindly, gently, overflowing with compassion, he draws the broken to himself and softly speaks words of healing. Oh so slowly bringing all the pieces back together again.

He opens his hands to show you his own scars and trades yours for his, taking your pain to heart. Who will devote themselves fully to the Lord? Only those who truly see him in the midst of their suffering. Who find him faithful and true in the light of all other betrayals. Who become acquainted with the comfort that he promises to give. Those who draw close find him drawing even closer, and are amazed that Someone so great would be capable of such intimacy. Fear may cause us initially to recoil from his touch, but fear dissipates as the power of his love overtakes all reason.

Who is he who loves us so? And who are we, that we should be loved so unconditionally? Why should he find us so attractive in even this most unlovely state? And yet, he does. Even in our need-iness, he finds us appealing. And now at last we can see it our-selves, our overwhelming need for him and him alone. Oh that everything else that surrounds could fade away! And indeed it does when we finally accept his invitation and lose ourselves in him.

Dear Heavenly Father, in the past I have not seen clearly enough your great love for me. But now that my love has fallen into ungrateful hands, I see the contrast. I ask your forgiveness for not seeking you as I should. As I reach out to you, please keep your promise and draw close to me.

I need your love, I crave your comfort. I admit that at times your love has not been real enough for me to grasp. Reveal yourself to me and let me feel your love. I need you now more than ever before. I need to know you, really know you, Lord. Show me how to love you more and hide my heart in you, where it will be kept safe.

Show me your goodness, even as you showed it to Moses. Let my countenance be changed by my encounter with you. Grant me a greater understanding of what I mean to you and who you are to me. Fill the empty places within me with yourself and let me rest com-plete in your arms. Help me to hide my self-esteem in you. Teach me who I am in light of your love. Help me to see myself as you see me and stand secure, believing that I am worthy to be loved because I belong to you. I understand that my worthiness comes from your hand and I accept it now, in Jesus' name. Amen.

Cover me
  like an old blanket that has been broken in
    by countless cold nights
      wrapped tightly
        to warm every cold crevice
      to ward off the chill
    that creeps between the cracks
  in the walls of my emotions.
Come and cover me
  like my favorite blanket
    soft and warm
      touchable and comforting
    a little worn from being clutched too much
  yet just enough to feel familiar.
Shut out everything else
  without, within, and in between
    let there be nothing else
      but us two
    the comforter
  and the one in need of comfort.
The coldness of others' hearts
  gives us both reasons
    for being where we are.

$\mathcal{I}$ Will Comfort

*The Lord will surely **comfort** Zion and will look with compassion*
on all her ruins; he will make her deserts like Eden,
her wastelands like the garden of the Lord.
Joy and gladness will be found in her,
thanksgiving and the sound of singing.
ISAIAH 51:3

$\mathcal{W}$ill you ever be joyful again?

Of course you will.

How do I know?

Because God said so.

While your heart writhes in discomfort, looking for the perfect spot to sink into, speak to it and command it to rest. To be still, allowing God to mold the place of consolation. Rest in his arms. Drink from the fountain of his love and be refreshed by his care for you. It is yours for the asking.

Yes, there are ruins. Shattered pieces of broken relationship littering your path. Shards of your spirit. Slivers of your heart. God sees them too. He longs to collect them and do what he does best. Mend and restore, making something out of seemingly nothing.

Will you step aside? Move out of the way? Allow him to do what you don't have the strength to do? You can trust him. You already have his word on that.

Yes, your heart is parched, a vast expanse of nothingness. You doubt its ability to bear fruit again, for there are no signs of life. Only cracks of disappointment. Crevices of broken promises.

Ruins of rejection and betrayal. The endless dryness of resignation. There is no line on the horizon, promising that tomorrow will be different. That it won't be a continuation of today.

Your eyes search for a sign, an oasis in the midst of your hopelessness. But don't look forward—look up! The rain is coming. It is in the hands of the One who promises to refresh the thirsty.

Remember, it is in the rest that new songs are birthed, so singing is certain. Don't try to rush the melody. Timing is everything. And all measures of time are in the Master Conductor's hands. Allow him to orchestrate your movements.

Simply listen. Yes, the song will come. From somewhere deep within your soul, softly peeking over the ridges of your pain, creeping forth carefully, covering the sting like a soothing oil. Just listen and go with the flow until you are carried by it. A symphony of praise. Unexpected, yet completely welcome.

Hmph, who would have thought it? There *is* life after heartbreak. Why? Simply because he said so.

Dear Heavenly Father, God of comfort, comfort me. Let your love be an easy chair I crawl into. Let me lose my pain in your arms. I am dry and weary from weeping. There are no tears left, only endless reminders of what caused my pain. I look to your hands like a hungry servant, waiting to be fed something that will cause the rumbling deep within to end.

And though I know it will take awhile, I only ask that you hold me and help me make it through this time. Assure me that this, too, will pass. That my grief won't be endless. Don't turn away from me and say I mourn too long. I need you—oh, how I need you—to wipe my wounds and bandage my heart. Stop the bleeding. Hold me and rock me. I am your child, you are my Father. I take refuge in the knowledge that I am safe as I abide in your shadow. Safe from further damage. Nearer to wholeness than I was before.

I commend all that I am in my brokenness into your care, in Jesus' name. Amen.

$\mathcal{I}$ Will Heal

∞

*"But I will restore you to health and **heal** your wounds,"*
declares the LORD, "because you are called an outcast,
Zion for whom no one cares."
JEREMIAH 30:17

$\mathcal{T}$he thought of wholeness seems out of reach in this place, far from the shores of fulfilling Love. Cast away, shattered, and forgotten, the word "whole" seems foreign. There is no ticket you can buy to take you there. God himself must carry you.

There is no expressway to this destination. It is a slow process. Inch by inch, step by step, you make your way, so that no wound might be left untouched. No damaged place passed over unnoticed. Healing from the inside out. Yes, this takes time. But God will do it. Gently he will cleanse your wounds and give them time to dry. He will bind the broken places and give them room to heal. Patiently waiting for each layer to knit together. God will breathe on the raw patches of your heart, cooling the inflammation of hurt, unforgiveness, bitterness, and despair.

Yes, let God himself carry you to the shores of Acceptance, where you will be free to believe that you are loved. Now and eternally loved. Rest in his promises, and let him bear you up. When you cannot rise and shake yourself, give him permission to assist you. His are the arms that you can trust. They will hold you secure until you reach your destination, and release you only when you are strong enough to stand again. Even then, he will be there to lean on in momentary lapses of weakness.

Yes, a day at a time, moment by moment. He will be there for you. Seeing you all the way through. This is his way. This is his promise.

Dear Heavenly Father, I surrender to your touch. I have tried to heal myself. After seeking help from the hands of friends, still I find myself wanting. Still very much in need of healing.

Come now and breathe on me. Breathe life back into me. Breathe love back into me. Love for you. Love for myself. Even love for those who hurt me. Let your love heal and renew me.

I am weak and tired. It is hard to have even the interest in being revived and still I fight to rise again. Help me. Speak to the dryness in my spirit and call it to arise. Help me to shake off this experience and move on. Hold me stable when I fear I won't be able to stand or go on. Be my rock, my fortress, my strong tower. Keep me from stumbling over past offenses and immediate fears. Heal even my memories, O God, and renew my hope in you for a new tomorrow, in Jesus' name. Amen.

38

ℐWill Strengthen You

∽◈∾

*The Lord will guide you always; he will **satisfy** your needs in
a sun-scorched land and will **strengthen** your frame. You will be
like a well-watered garden, like a spring whose waters never fail.*

ISAIAH 58:11

ℋ re you feeling dry and lifeless? Are you tired to the very
core of your soul?

Trust him. You've always done things your way. Now it's time
to let him direct your path.

Put your hand in his. Let him lead you beside still waters and
through green pastures that offer the kind of sustenance you
need to regain your strength. He knows your needs. Knows them
better than you do, knows the needs even you don't know about.
He knows the secret places in your soul that need to be fed. The
wasted places that need to be nourished.

We are but dust. God knows this. He knows the frailty of our
frame, and yet he makes divine compensation for our human
deficiencies. Without judging, without scolding, he simply turns
us gently back on course. Feeding us words of restoration and
care.

Yes, he leads us. Sometimes forward, sometimes back. Forward
to new pastures. Changing our diet from the familiar "comfort
food" to deeper truths, richer bread, heartier meat. Nourish-
ment to make the blood thicker, to add marrow to the bones and
flesh to the body.

Sometimes God leads us backward, retracing our steps to find
choice morsels we've dropped along the way. Some we have
dropped accidentally, not realizing how vital they were to our

spiritual health; others were dropped purposely, because we simply were not ready to eat. But God wants us to finish everything on our plate. Even the things we don't like.

Just as grains and roughage provide the fiber we need in life to strengthen us for the long haul, so it is with life's lessons. As difficult as they may be, these lessons are steppingstones to a higher place. So eat what God extends to you for the journey. Feeding from his hand, you will be strengthened, and thereby established, never to be bowed over again.

Dear Heavenly Father, I come to you empty, hungry, longing to be filled. I admit that my spiritual diet has suffered. My strength is depleted and I am running low on faith. Feed me, nurture me with your Word, and let me gain power from your Spirit.

Forgive me for all of the times I sought satisfaction from other sources. In attempting to nourish myself, I have gone hungry. I have come to understand that only you can satisfy my every need.

Now that I know nothing else will suffice, I come to you with my hands ready to receive from you. Help me to build myself from the inside out. Grant me the firm foundation of your faithfulness and the pillars of your wisdom, that I might be a strong temple of honor for your name's sake, in Jesus' name. Amen.

I woke up this morning
   put one foot in front of the other
     automatically
      mechanically
       making my way down the same road
  I've traveled before.
Now here you stand
  in the center of my path
    causing me to doubt
      my customary direction,
    showing me another way.
I am paralyzed
  afraid to go forward,
    afraid to go back.
I stand rooted to the spot
  waiting for some guarantee,
    some promise
      to convince me that your way is best
    but you offer me none of these.
You simply say,
  "My child, trust me."

39

I Will Direct You

ᗛᗒ

Whether you turn to the right or to the left, your ears will hear
*a **voice** behind you, saying, "**This** is the **way**; walk in it."*
ISAIAH 30:21

*W*here do you go from here?

Go the way the Spirit leads you.

No matter how many mistakes you've made. How many disappointments have assaulted you, rocked you, and left you feeling unstable. Unsure of which direction to take... or of whether you ought to move *at all.*

Listen as the Holy Spirit gently instructs you. Open your ears to hear and know what the Spirit of the Lord is saying. "Come, my child, come and rest awhile ... there now, let us move on ... turn right here, not left."

You see, you will receive more than marching orders; he will also give *resting* orders. When to stop. When to go. You know, there is a time for every purpose. He will give directions for disinfecting your wounds and healing your ills, and for restoring lost territory in your heart. Detailed, minute instructions of how to get from this place to higher ground.

Believe me, God will always ask you to do something completely new to get to the next level of blessing. He will call you out of your comfort zone to discover another area of his grace. Perhaps he wants you to alter and rearrange some things, to make room for what's in store.

Out with the old, in with the new, according to his prescription and design. It's time to cast down old ideas and habits. Time for the Holy Spirit to speak renewal to your mind and transformation to your life. And if you are wise, you will listen and be changed. Changed into a new you, with a new attitude, a new view, a new grasp on life. Attracting new people, new things, new opportunities into your midst. Yes, this is your life. Who would have ever thought you'd make it to this place? And yet, by the leading of the Lord, you have. Welcome to your new beginning!

Dear Heavenly Father, I have exhausted the counsel of friends, family, and other loved ones. Now I find myself back where I started— waiting on you. Though initially their suggestions sounded good and I was even able to draw some measure of comfort from them, still I find myself at a loss as to where I go from here.

Lord, I know that you hold all my tomorrows, and only you know what the future truly holds. You hold the map of my life in your hands. You know my beginning and my end. Take my hand and lead me in the way that I should take. Speak to me of the future and give me instruction. Show me where I went wrong and correct my thinking. Dispel my own incorrect assumptions and the lies of the enemy.

Holy Spirit, lead me. Show me the way that I should take. Teach me all I need to know to attain victory and secure it. Grant me your wisdom, that I might walk with prudence and discretion. Lord, I am ready now to do things your way. Guide me into the liberty that you have ordained for me, in Jesus' name. Amen.

$\mathcal{I}$Will Restore You

∞

*This is what the Lord says: "I will **restore** the fortunes of Jacob's tents and have compassion on his dwellings; the city will be rebuilt on her ruins, and the palace will stand in its proper place."*
JEREMIAH 30:18

$\mathcal{I}$t's inevitable, really. The things that brew inside of us will, one way or the other, make their way to the surface and spill over into the other areas of our lives. Relationships that leave us feeling emotionally bankrupt can cause us to make decisions subconsciously to threaten our own financial security. The inability to think clearly about a relationship can affect our ability to function at work or in other areas of life. When the heart suffers, every aspect of life feels the pain.

This is one of the ways that the spirit of robbery is able to accomplish some of his best work. As he paralyzes us, making our world a shambles of disorganization and lack of focus, many important things fall by the wayside.

And then the Lord comes, just as he promised. Like a breath of fresh air he comes, and gazes on our disarray with eyes that understand our dishevelment. Slowly he begins to pick up the pieces. Whispering sweet words of encouragement and promise, he refills the coffers of our heart with the riches of his love.

We are not paupers! No, no, no, we are coheirs of a royal inheritance, for we are the beloved! Our King will not leave us unadorned. He replaces all that the enemy of our souls has stolen with treasures far more magnificent. Gifts intended by his good pleasure to enrich not only our lives, but the lives of those all around us.

But he does not stop there. Having restored our finery, he turns to the broken places in our spirits and gently, sliver by sliver, begins the rebuilding of who we are. Some pieces he hands to us. We must cooperate in this work—he will not do it alone. *So "pick up a brick, sister" and get busy!* For it is in the process of re-building that we grow more familiar with our foundation. That we become firmly established in truths from which we will never again be shaken. That our boundaries become more cohesive, able to stand firm in the face of opposing elements. When at last he finishes the task, the Lord stands back and admires his hand-iwork. You are complete. Whole, tall, and strong. Like a palace, resplendent, a wonder to behold. A temple made for God's glory. And in that knowledge you take your place, allowing his light to shine forth. You are no longer unstable, no longer uninhabit-able. Finally you are all that you were called and created to be—the house of the Lord.

Dear Heavenly Father, you have promised to restore the years of my life that the locusts and the cankerworm have destroyed. I have wasted so much time, precious time that I feel I have lost forever. I don't quite comprehend how you can restore what is already gone, but I choose to trust you.

All I see before me are ruins, but you see a whole temple where you abide. I see shattered pieces of my heart, but you see a glittering jewel that you call your own. Where I see empty tomorrows, you see days bright and filled with promise.

Change my vision to match your own, Lord. I long to see what you see. I long for you to show yourself strong on my behalf and redeem my situation. Fill my world with your restoration. Let my life be a testimony of your grace, and I will be careful to give you all the praise, all the glory, and declare your works to all that surround me, in Jesus' name. Amen.

$\mathcal{I}$ Will Exchange Your Garments

The Spirit of the Sovereign Lord is on me, because the Lord has
anointed me to … bind up the brokenhearted, to proclaim freedom
for the captives and release for the prisoners … to comfort all who
mourn, and provide for those who grieve in Zion—to bestow on them
a crown of beauty instead of ashes, the oil of gladness instead of
mourning, and a garment of praise instead of a spirit of despair.
ISAIAH 61:1-3

$\mathcal{G}$od can't help himself. He must fix what is broken. Bind
what is separated. Fill what is empty. Set free what is
bound. He is driven by the Spirit, compelled to come and see
about you. This is a sovereign demand, placed upon the divine
for the sake of the finite.

Yes, for our sakes the Lord is bound by his own promises to rescue us from the labor of pain. To touch, embrace, and comfort us.
To rescue us from the taunts of shame and rejection, the lashes of
betrayal and upheaval. To transform ugliness into a thing of
beauty that crowns your understanding and lifts your head.

Gently he bathes us, casting off the old tattered garments of
grief and despair. They are too heavy for us, our shoulders were
not designed for that kind of weight. He brings lighter garments,
an easier yoke, just as he said he would.

And then there is the oil. The rich perfume of it fills your new
garments and rides the wind around you, drawing others with its
contagious scent. Joy is like that, you know. Light enough not to
offend, yet pungent enough to make its presence known. This is

the most precious of gifts for those who have wept too long.

Yes, he will let you have your cry. But only for a night. We have his word. Weeping may endure for a night…. However, when the Son comes, he extends his joy to you, in exchange for your sadness. In the light of his love there are no more dark corners in which to hide your tears. And so he takes them and scatters them to the wind, extinguishing the heat of your former trials, bringing on the dusk, propelling you toward a new day.

He does this because he must. He is bound by his own word, by the design of his own omniscience, to compensate for our weaknesses in this way. He has called us all to be perfect, even as he is perfect. And in the light of all he bestows upon us, we are.

Dear Heavenly Father, my garments are heavy from the weight of my tears. I have drenched them in the midst of my wonderings and whys, in the midst of my unanswered issues and questions.

But now I am ready for a change. No more questions—I trust you to answer them. I choose to exercise the authority you have given me through the name of Jesus and I speak to my soul. I cast off sadness and heaviness, depression, and despair. I embrace gladness and joy, peace, and fulfillment. I break the bondage of rejection, anger, unforgiveness, and bitterness from myself and declare myself free to love and give again.

Father, I choose to walk in cooperation with you as you rebuild my life. I will not return to unvictorious habits, or get caught up in repetitive relational cycles. I will follow you into the victory that you have declared awaits me. Lead me there now, in Jesus' name. Amen.

$\mathcal{I}$ Will Give You Good Things
∞

Bless the Lord, O my soul, and forget none of his benefits; Who
pardons all your iniquities; Who heals all your diseases; Who redeems
your life from the pit; Who crowns you with lovingkindness and
compassion; Who satisfies your years with good things,
So that your youth is renewed like the eagle's.
PSALM 103:2-5, NASB

$\mathcal{L}$ook to God's hands. They come loaded with good things. Forgiveness, healing, wholeness, release from all that has held you down. Love, compassion, understanding, restoration … oh, too many things to name. The hands of the Lord are full. Brimming and running over with benefits to share.

And here we sit with empty hands, grieving the loss of so much less. Reach out your hands and begin to receive. Let him give you a make-over, get rid of all that keeps your heart sick. Let him lift you and set you where you can walk without stumbling. Stand still and let him dress you from head to toe. Allow him to design what truly suits you. Love, favor, and goodness. Mmm, you wear it well and he knows it. Even when you don't.

That knowledge is key. He knows our own hearts better than we do. He knows what it takes to truly satisfy us. So don't spurn his advances when he comes bearing something different, something unfamiliar. We have grown too used to disappointment. Allow him to surprise you.

He will, you know. He can't help himself. It is woven into every part of his eternal nature to fulfill us with every touch, every encounter. We turn away, afraid of happiness, so complacent that we stay where we are, even when it hurts.

But *he* won't allow us to stay that way. He troubles the waters of our souls and nudges our spirits to remember all that he's done before. To anticipate all he will do if we let him. On that note, dare to take his hand and examine all that is there. It's all for you. And it's all good.

Dear Heavenly Father, I thank you for the power that abides in me. Now help me to use it. Help me to open my hands to receive from you. I admit that I have tried to dictate which gifts you should give me, but I surrender now. You know what is best. I cast off all doubts and I embrace with faith all you have in store for me.

Father, I am walking in anticipation, expecting that my heart will be blessed by your visitation. Give me eyes to see the surprises planned by your hand all around me as I make my way through my day. May I take no kindness for granted. No happening as mere coincidence. I will see all these things as wonderful benefits of belonging to you. Thank you for your blessings, but most of all, thank you for your love. In Jesus' name, I glorify you. Amen.

I have been left by many
  cast aside
      replaced
          or kept waiting
  and now you come
bearing a different promise
of "to have and to hold forever."
I close my eyes
  and try to imagine it
      and though I find it a desirable prospect
          it feels foreign to my heart.
      before I speak you say you understand
and I fear what you cause my heart to feel
  and then you touch me from where you stand
      and my spirit quivers.
There is something about your touch
  that tells me I can believe you.
      I wrap my arms around myself
          and rehearse your words
      again and again …
"I will never leave you nor forsake you."

$\mathcal{I}$ Will Never Leave You

∞

*God has said, "**Never** will I **leave** you; **never** will I forsake you."*
HEBREWS 13:5

$\mathcal{Y}$ou've heard those words before, haven't you? And yet, this is the one time that they are true. God is the only constant in the equation between you and him. He was here before you, and he will be here after you step over the threshold of man's finite measure of his space that we call time.

Even there, he will follow you. To the other side of life as we know it. To the gates of heaven. To the brink of hell. He will hem you in with his love. No, he will never leave you. He cannot, because he is everywhere. To the left, the right. There is nowhere you can go to flee his presence.

His love knows no boundaries, and it will go to any length to reach you. Ever burning, ever reaching, beckoning you to come in out of the cold, dark night of bad choices and unconscious mistakes. Extending arms to cover you from the rain and keep you safe. He is a persistent lover. Loving you in spite of yourself, because he is unchanging.

He cannot leave you, because he cannot be detached from himself. You are a part of his body. He will not forsake you. He promises to surpass your dreams and be the fulfillment of all that you seek. Yes, he alone will love you without measure or constriction. Without deadlines. Without conditions. In spite of you, he will stay.

He is everywhere. In the air you breathe. The song you sing.

The words you speak. The moves you make. He is the everything of our being! So leaving is not an option to him. He has promised. And he cannot tell a lie.

Dear Heavenly Father, I have been hurt and disappointed in the past, but now I am putting my heart in your hands for safekeeping.

Today, I choose to believe that you will keep your promises to me. That you will always be there for me. That you will not allow my heart to suffer any longer from the lack of true love. I am yours and you are mine eternally.

I look forward to the day when I will finally be one with you and know you as you truly are. Until then I will walk in the knowledge of your love for me, listening for your word, awaiting your visitation. I will rest. I will rejoice because your banner over me reminds me of your love, the love I've always longed for. Lord, thank you for being there. I bless your name, in Jesus' Name. Amen.

$\mathcal{I}$ Will Give You a New Name
∞

No longer will they call you Deserted, or name your land Desolate.
But you will be called Hephzibah, and your land Beulah; for the
Lord will take delight in you, and your land will be married.... and
you will be called Sought After, The City No Longer Deserted.
ISAIAH 62:4, 12

$\mathcal{B}$ecause he is the great I Am, you are. You are all that you
long to be, because he is everything you need. A husband,
a lover, a comforter, a confidant, and friend. He will not allow you
to suffer disgrace or desolation. The Lord himself will draw close
and claim you as his own. He will write his own name upon you
and call all others to agree with him.

The glow of a new bride will light your countenance, even the
way you carry yourself will change. You will walk with the air of a
woman who is possessed by her lover. Confident, fulfilled, at
peace with herself, her Maker, her world. No air of sadness will
hang like a cloud over your disposition, heralding your alone-
ness. Quite the contrary. It will be clearly evident to all concerned
that you are loved. Loved and possessed by One who is desirable
and good.

You have not been forsaken. Those who had unloving intentions toward you have been displaced by the One who truly
loves you. Passionately. Deeply. Unselfishly. He has gone to prepare a place for you, a mansion with rooms unnumbered. All of
heaven stands on alert, awaiting your arrival. A banquet is being
prepared. The streets have been paved with gold, and jewels

adorn everything to delight your eye.

In the meantime, he greets you with whispers of love every morning. He soothes you to sleep each night with his promises of faithfulness. Throughout the day he showers you with constant reminders of his love—supplying your needs and delighting your heart.

He is so thoughtful, his thoughts toward you outnumber the grains of sand in all the earth. So loving, he reached out to you while you were yet unlovable. So generous, he has given his very life for you.

No, you are not alone. You belong to the lover of all lovers. How special is that? Wrap yourself in that knowledge and let it keep you warm.

You are because he is. Remember that and let it change the way you look at the world. His love will beautify you and draw those to you who seek light, true love, and all that is lovely. You see, we attract what we are. And you are delightful, loved, and sought after in him.

Dear Heavenly Father, you make me feel brand new. I stand in agreement with your word that I am loved. I feel so privileged to know that you delight in me. I thank you that my identity—my personal worth—has been settled by you.

I am not what I think of myself. I am what you say that I am. I receive your word that I am whole, free, and loved. I am betrothed to you. A bride made worthy by the blood of the Lamb. He has paid a ransom for my hand, and I gladly accept his proposal. Father, if you loved me enough to give your only begotten Son for me, I, too, am willing to sacrifice my life for you.

Lord, thank you for all that you have done for me. You have ransomed me, cleansed me, healed me, crowned me, counseled me, comforted me, led me, carried me … O Lord, you've done so much. You've been so good! Thank you for being all that I have sought in other men. You have been a friend, a brother, a provider, a confidant, the lover of my soul, and more. Today I delight in you and all that you are. I pray that every day that I live I will do something that will bring a smile to your face, in Jesus' name. Amen.

The Peace

No matter what happens in our world or how we feel about ourselves, there are eight things (eight being the number significant of new beginnings) that I know about myself—and that *you* ought to know about *yourself!*

☐ *I know that I am in transition* because God will not allow me to remain in the same place.

☐ *I know that I am better for my experiences,* no matter how bad it felt at the time, because wisdom is gained through pain.

☐ *I know that I am free* because God has extended deliverance to me and I have chosen to seize it.

☐ *I know that I am whole* because God will not leave me broken.

☐ *I know that I am secure in his arms.* My heart is safe in my Father's care.

☐ *I know that I am desirable,* not because of who I am on the outside, but because of who resides within me.

☐ *I know that I am loved,* eternally, fiercely, and passionately by the author of love himself.

☐ *I know that I belong to someone,* and no one can snatch me from his hand but me myself.

These are my confessions as I pick myself up and begin again. "It is well with my soul," because I have his promises to cling to.

Make them yours, too. Repeat them again and again until they become a part of you. These things keep me rooted in my faith, help me believe that tomorrow will be better than today. These things compel me to keep moving forward, no matter how sluggish I may feel in my spirit.

I press forward, hoping against hope and all other opposition, straining to get to the other side of my circumstance. I am confident that what God has spoken, he will be faithful to perform.

No need for a money-back guarantee, he will deliver. This is my confidence. This gives me calm in the midst of the storm. Though the waves may billow high, I will grip the sides of the boat and ride it out, awaiting the inevitable.

Yes, the storm will end, the winds will cease, and every evidence of the raging squall will vanish to the naked eye. And I will fall back into the arms of Jesus, who sits calmly in the bow, smiling at the waves. "Peace, be still," he whispers to me as I fall asleep.

As I said, these are my personal confessions. They can be yours, too.

45

I Am in Transition

⤖

Then your light will break forth like the dawn, and your healing
will quickly appear; then your righteousness will go before you,
*and the **glory** of the Lord will be your rear guard.*

ISAIAH 58:8

Turn toward the morning and embrace the Son. The darkness is behind me. I am moving forward, toward my new beginning. For every time my heart has been broken, my spirit crushed, I have been resurrected to a new life.

Change is not easy. Familiar habits forced from their niches leave vacuums of discomfort for a little while, but eventually this too shall pass, leaving no evidence of former folly or transgression.

The closer I draw to the light, the more clearly I see my own healing. The presence of God surrounds me and assures me of a better future. With a renewed sense of purpose and destiny, I take heed and move on toward the promised victory. Clocking landmarks along the way, I determine not to return to this place. I will seek higher ground. I will follow the call of God.

I will no longer despair over where I've been. My future looks nothing like my past, for God will not allow it. He does not want me to remain the same. He challenges me to spread reluctant wings and fly. *Come higher. Come higher. Be changed from glory to glory.*

Wanting to shine like him, I submit to the flames that purge. I want to be pure gold, a twenty-four karat reflection of his face. Shifting, turning, I let go of debris. Of the old. Of the past. And I reach to embrace a handsome stranger called Overcomer. He extends his hands to relieve me of my load. Yes, truly I have been made fruitful in the land of my affliction. I am equipped to finish the journey.

Dear Heavenly Father, I trust you to write my tomorrows and file my yesterdays in a place that will not harm me. I will await your direction.

Give me the courage. Though I long for freedom and victory, I am afraid to venture into such unknown territory. I have forgotten how to laugh, truly laugh and kiss the wind, so bowed over have I been in my despair.

You are the lifter of my head. Raise me now and lead me on. I am ready. Ready for change. Ready for deliverance. Ready to experience the fullness of the joy and peace that you have ordained for me. Yes, I am ready. Lead the way, in Jesus' name. Amen.

$\mathcal{I}$ Am Better for the Experience

∽∞∾

We also rejoice in our sufferings, because we know that
suffering produces perseverance; perseverance, character;
and character, hope. And hope does not disappoint us,
because God has poured out his love into our hearts
by the Holy Spirit, whom he has given us.

ROMANS 5:3-5

There was a time, not too long ago, when you couldn't have told me that anything good could come out of this. But now it is clearly evident. I am wiser for this experience, bitter as it was.

Though God heals memories, he will not allow us to forget and lose the lesson. No, I will place all that I have learned in a file that will be opened only to refer to when wisdom is needed, or to counsel another who has haplessly found herself on the same path I once trod. If that happens, when that happens, I will gently lead this suffering one to safer ground, comforting with the comfort with which I was comforted.

Truly I am better for my brokenness. I recognize danger faster. Sense the unfruitful more readily. I now know the wisdom of denying myself pleasantries that will only waste my time, my heart, and my emotions. I take better care of my heart. I no longer leave it carelessly in the wrong places. I choose to be more discerning. Trusting only God, and loving only those he releases me to love.

I am kinder to myself, understanding that God says I am worthy of more than what I previously settled for. I have learned that I am free to give his love away, but not my own. Committed into his safekeeping is the best place for all that I hold dear.

At last I can exhale. I do not fear disgrace or rejection because I keep well within the boundaries of his wisdom. I no longer make foolish moves, but wait for the finger of God to chart my course. And in his leading I rest. No longer stumbling, I move onward and upward, strong and sure that my testimony has a happy ending.

Dear Heavenly Father, thank you for your patience. Thank you for bringing me through the process I needed, so that I might grow into the image of the woman you have called me to be. Though I balked at the journey, you were faithful, and now I welcome the cloud you send by day and the fire you send at night. I will follow you, even when I'm weary, because your path is sure and it leads me to my good.

And so I follow after you with my hands open to all that you bring, even the chastening that bears the peaceable fruit of righteousness.

Take me, make me, mold me as you will, so that I will be an instrument of praise to your glory and the benefit of others. Let them see your hand at work in my life, giving me victory in unexpected places. I pray that my suffering would be used in a way that will make a difference. By the power of your Spirit, take what the enemy of my soul meant for evil and turn it around for the good of all, in Jesus' name. Amen.

$\mathcal{I}$ Am Free

∞

So if the Son sets you free, you will be free indeed.
JOHN 8:36

There I was, like a kitten trying to untangle a mess of yarn, trying to find one end of the chain that had wrapped itself around my heart. I was just beginning to wonder if I would ever be free of the pain, when my thoughts were interrupted by your glorious presence.

You saw that my heart was in trouble, and you rescued me. Came down, broke the chains, and set me free. You knew that I would never be able to free myself—not by might, not by power, not by emotional manipulation or intellectual rationalization ... no, simply by the Spirit *doing his* work.

He is at work even today. Touching, prodding, digging, cleansing, not stopping until he is finished, the Spirit labors even while we sleep. Breathing fresh life back into members too weary to stretch. Exercising spiritual muscles atrophied from lack of use as we try to solve our problems in the flesh. Stirring up the Word. Rehearsing God's promises to us, even in our dreams. Singing songs in the Spirit and in the understanding until we join in....

No, the Spirit will not let you rest in your despair. He grabs an arm and coaxes you toward the finish line. *Come on, come on. To she that endures, the prize will be given.* I can smell the victory. Feel the freedom on my skin like a cooling breeze, washing over inflamed emotions that are extinguished only to be refreshed by the quiet that true rest brings.

He's got it all in control. I don't have to hold on any longer. No more holding on to what was holding me. Who held who, anyway? Now I finally see. And so I let go, and freefall back into his arms. I've got to laugh as I feel the release! Ooo-wee, now *this* is what I mean. To paraphrase a great man who knew the difference, "I'm free at last!"

Dear Heavenly Father, thank you for setting me free. I will not return to the place of bondage or take on the yoke of slavery again. No longer will I cast my pearls before swine. I will leave them in your hands. I have learned that true freedom abides within your care. This is where I desire to dwell at all times.

Allow me to dwell in the secret place of the Most High, the shadow of the Almighty. It feels so cool, it smells so sweet there. Take me and hide me under your wings. Lord, let my heart beat to your rhythm, and sing your freedom song. Songs of peace and deliverance that set the captive free. And as I surrender all that I am to you, let your song become mine, in Jesus' name. Amen.

$\mathcal{I}$Am Whole

∞

Consider it pure joy, my brothers, whenever you face trials of many
kinds, because you know that the testing of your faith develops
perseverance. Perseverance must finish its work so that you may be
mature and complete, not lacking anything.

JAMES 1:2-4

$\mathcal{I}$ know more now than I did before. More about myself.
More about men. More about God and his grace. This was
a test, and I believe I've passed it. I'm still standing, that's for sure.
That has to mean something. Others have withered and died but
I'm still here.

I am told that I look different. I should. Now all the puzzle
pieces fit. I can see the whole picture. I have been through something and come out on the other side. True revelation always
brings transformation. If I haven't been changed by the experience, then I didn't "get it." And I do want to "get it" because I do
not want to repeat the lesson again. It was not fun, though it must
have been necessary.

Why? The reason escapes me just now. But in time I know that
I will understand all things fully. For now I will learn what I have
been able to grasp and use it to my benefit. Growing another
inch. Walking another mile in Jesus' shoes. No pain, no gain.

There is no way around the lessons of life, and they will not go
away. You will remain in the same space, doing the same exercise
over again and again, until you complete your course and grad-
uate to the next level. You cannot cheat. You cannot borrow from
the past paper. When God gives you a clean slate, don't write the
same thing on it again. I learned that lesson well. In the learning

I find wholeness, health, and strength. My issues are settled at last. I've made peace with myself. I am all right with me. The fight is over, and now I find I carry less and yet I have so much more.

Dear Heavenly Father, thank you for loving me enough to allow me to make mistakes in order to learn my lessons. Thank you for using those lessons to fashion me into a work of art. I now see your wisdom, though there was a time when I questioned why you were allowing me to suffer so much.

I know there will be other lessons ahead of me. Abide with me and help me to pass every test. For every test makes me more complete, shaping me into a vessel for your glory. Remind me by your Spirit in the difficult times that you will not allow me to go through more than I can bear. You know me so much better than I know myself.

Thank you for pushing me beyond my comfort zone of endurance. Just when I think I will break I am amazed to discover that you have given me strength, just when I thought I was fresh out.

Thanks to your faithfulness and patience, I am whole. I am full. I am an overcomer, in Jesus' name. Amen.

$\mathcal{I}$ Am Secure

∞

Yet I am not ashamed, because I know whom I have believed,
*and am convinced that he is able to guard **what** I have*
entrusted to him for that day.
2 TIMOTHY 1:12

$\mathcal{M}$y heart is safe in the hands of my Savior. I no longer wield it carelessly, or bestow it too generously on the undeserving and undiscerning. I have placed it where it should have been in the first place. In the hands of my Lord.

Tenderly he cradles my heart like a precious jewel, until I finally see its worth reflected in his eyes. The longer I gaze, the more I see his passionate love for me. His protection. His infinite care for all that has been yielded completely to him.

I am sheltered safe within the arms of my God. Under his watchful eye I have no fear. I am a well-kept woman in every way. I am his and he is mine. Nothing can pluck me from his protection.

I am possessed. Ransomed and owned by the Master of Everything. He has paved the way to his throne and given me access, to make my requests known. I can boldly enter and hide myself there in the light of his glory, where no evil can touch me. "I'm going high where the devil can't go."

I am in my Father's hand, and none will dare try to touch me there. My heart is sheltered from the eyes of those who harbor unclean intentions, for they do not like the light. No prowler, deceiver, or abuser, no one treacherous or rash dares to venture near the Holy One. It is too great a risk. The hand of God shields me from those who would take advantage. He is my rock, my fortress, my strong tower. In him alone do I trust.

Dear Heavenly Father, I have learned to expect nothing from man and everything from you. I know that I can trust you with my heart. You won't drop it, damage it, or disregard it. I know that you watch over my every need and are attentive to every cry. I can rest secure in your keeping.

Help me, Lord, to await your word before I share my heart with others. Though I may not always be able to discern the hearts of men, I know that you do. Let me not grow anxious. May I always trust your direction above my own emotions. All that matters is that my heart remains open to your call. Preserve me and keep me according to your promise, in Jesus' name. Amen.

$\mathcal{I}$ Am Desirable

∞

*I belong to **my** lover, and his **desire** is for me.... For your Maker is your husband—the Lord Almighty is his name—the Holy One of Israel is your Redeemer; he is called the God of all the earth.*
SONG OF SONGS 7:10; ISAIAH 54:5

Who am I, that the King of Kings and the Lord of Lords desires me? Who indeed? I am simply me. Fearfully and wonderfully made.

God held his breath when he formed me in my mother's womb. Ever so lovingly and carefully he etched out my features. Tenderly he leaned down from the portals of heaven and breathed upon me, giving me life. And as I basked in the safety of my mother's womb, his spirit hovered over me, whispering the plans he had for me. Plans for good and not for evil, to give me a future and an expected end.

What is my expected end? Even this I know—to be betrothed to the Ultimate Bridegroom. The Prince of Peace, the Lion of Judah, the soon-coming Conqueror. His name is Wonderful, his name is Jesus. He is my intended. I love him because he first loved me. He chose me before the beginning of time to be his very own. He sought me out, called me beautiful, and paid a king's ransom for my life. And when all others made me feel unlovely, he came, calling me the pearl of great price, asking for my hand.

Even now in spite of all I say and do, his thoughts toward me outnumber the grains of sand upon the earth. He longs after me and anticipates our meeting when he comes again. He is jealous over me, passionate, and consuming. Possessive and true. He alone is deserving of my undivided attention.

And yet I wonder. Why does he love me so? Why am I his desire? It is a mystery I cannot comprehend. But this much I do know. He has never been shy on stating it. I am his desire, and he is mine.

Dear Heavenly Father, thank you for making me feel beautiful. To be desired by a king is such a great honor—and I have settled for so much less. To know that I have your love, your affection, your attention is an overwhelming thought.

Rebuild my esteem and let me see myself as you see me. Thank you for showing me who I really am. How much my love and my life is worth to you. I choose to embrace the truth that I am precious and worthy. Your love has made me lovely. Your passion has made me glow. You presence has transformed me into a vessel of honor that draws the admiration of others. Thank you, Father, for dressing me so magnificently. Continue to shine forth from me each and every day, and let every flaw that I possess be hidden in your light, in Jesus' name. Amen.

$\mathcal{I}$ Am Loved

∞

Who shall separate us from the love of Christ? … I am convinced
that neither death nor life, neither angels nor demons, neither the
present nor the future, nor any powers, neither height nor depth,
nor anything else in all creation, will be able to separate us from
the love of God that is in Christ Jesus our Lord.
ROMANS 8:35, 38

$\mathcal{I}$ am his. I am his. Totally and completely his. Mmmm. The thought is sweet, lingering like heady incense. It wafts through the air, a vivid reminder of my beloved's presence. There is no doubt, he has been here. His essence, unseen yet undeniable, remains firmly fixed in my imagination. Oh yes, he has definitely been here.

Such is the Spirit of God. It hovers attentively, guarding his own. Passionate over his loved one. Nothing will interrupt our union. He will allow no other to come between us. He has pledged himself to me eternally, and he will keep his vow. Separate yet together, time is not strong enough to break the bond we share.

I will wait for him. And yet, his presence surrounds me in the wind, in the song of the air, the rumble of thunder, the warmth of night. It is all a continuous and passionate dialogue reminding me of his closeness.

The circle of his love is unending, hemming me in behind and before, keeping me in the center of his heart. His banner over me is love. His care stretches beneath my feet and bears me up. I am carried by his love for me. I am loved! No matter what anyone says or does—or doesn't say or do. I am loved. Fiercely, passionately, unwaveringly, continuously loved.

My heart pounds. The magnitude of his love for me takes my breath away. I am not alone. I have someone to watch over me, to love me as I have never been loved. To love me the way I've always dreamed of being loved. Why did it take me so long to get to this glorious place? To see what has always been true. I am deeply and overwhelmingly loved.

Dear Heavenly Father, my heart is so full. I weep tears of joy at the realization of your great love for me. The thought warms me so deliciously. I am loved! Fancy that! Little ole me, who has felt so unworthy, so unlovely, overlooked, abused, and discarded. You find me worthy of picking up, cleaning off, dressing, and loving. Not just loving, but loooooving, thoroughly, through, and through. It is such a new and wonderful feeling.

Hey, you know what, Lord? I love you too! I pray you accept my love, as small as it may be in comparison to the greatness of your heart, in Jesus' name. Amen.

$\mathcal{I}$ Belong to Someone
⋘

I will betroth you to me forever; I will betroth you in righteousness and justice, in love and compassion. I will betroth you in faithfulness, and you will acknowledge the Lord. I will plant her for myself in the land; I will show my love to the one I called "Not my loved one." I will say to those called "Not my people," "You are my people"; and they will say, "You are my God."

HOSEA 2:19-20, 23

$\mathcal{W}$ ho said I was single? Not true. I am betrothed. Like Mary was betrothed to Joseph. I am waiting for my bridegroom to come. I have his promise and I know that he will be on time. He always is. He has proven to be trustworthy.

Faithful and true is my beloved. Not leery of love, for he *is* love. Love in the flesh. He saturates me with it and waters me with his compassion. I feel my roots go deep, guided by his faithfulness. I am settled. I am here to stay. I belong to someone. Not just anyone. I belong to him. The one who holds forever in his hands. And he has pledged all his tomorrows to me.

And in the moment that we embrace, the circle will be complete. I will be home at last. In the arms of the one who loves me most. Caught up into eternity where love will abide forever unbroken. This is his promise to me. And he cannot lie.

No, I am not alone. I am his. He is mine. We are one. Living and breathing inside of each other. Two souls united. Bound by cords that cannot be broken. Spoken vows that cannot be retrieved.

We stand before the Father approved. Grafted into the vine. We are forever intertwined. And heaven stands witness. I am wedded. Married. Possessed by the Lover of my Soul. I am a lot of things in him, but alone is not one of them. I belong to some-one.

Dear Heavenly Father, it is so good to know that I belong to you. You are my saving grace. For every moment that the tempter tries to deceive me with loneliness, I pray that you will make our nearness real to me. Wrap your arms around me and keep me warm. Hide me in your heart and write your name across it. Let me be a walking testimony of your ownership of my life.

Today I choose to turn away from my past and from the things and people who keep me bound. I embrace you and the freedom you offer. As I yield to the lordship of Jesus in every area of my life, I believe that you can make me whole again.

I open my hands to you now and say, "Take my life, I am yours." Prepare me to be a sanctuary, a place where you are pleased to dwell.

Lord, I love you so much. Thank you for redeeming me and choosing me for your Son. Make me a worthy bride that will bring pleasure to his heart. Until then let your love shine in me and fill me with the joy I have been longing for, in Jesus' name. Amen.

"Though the mountains be shaken and the hills be removed, yet my unfailing love for you will not be shaken nor my covenant of peace be removed,"
says the Lord, who has compassion on you.

ISAIAH 54:10

Recommended Reading

Betrayal's Baby
by P.B. Wilson
New Dawn Publishing Company

The Blessings of Brokenness
by Charles Stanley
Zondervan Publishing House

Lord, Heal My Hurts
by Kay Arthur
Questar Publications

When Forgiveness Doesn't Make Sense
by Robert Jeffress
Waterbrook Press

Woman Thou Art Loosed
by T. D. Jakes
Destiny Image